GHOSTLY BEACONS:

HAUNTED LIGHTHOUSES OF NORTH AMERICA

GHOSTLY BEACONS:

Therese Lanigan-Schmidt

Whitford Press

A Division of Schiffer Publishing
4880 Lower Valley Rd.
Atglen, PA 19310 USA

Cover Design Bruce Waters
Book Design Blair Loughrey
Type set in Souvenir LT BT/Zurich

ISBN: 0-7643-1114-X
Printed in China

Published by Whitford Press
4880 Lower Valley Road
Atglen, PA 19310
Phone: (610) 593-1777; Fax: (610) 593-2002
E-mail: Schifferbk@aol.com
Please visit our web site catalog at
WWW.SCHIFFERBOOKS.COM

We are always looking for people to write books
on new and related subjects. If you have an idea
for a book, please contact us at the above
address.

This book may be purchased from the publisher.
Include $3.95 for shipping. Please try your
bookstore first.
You may write for a free catalog.

In Europe, Schiffer books are distributed by
Bushwood Books
6 Marksbury Ave. Kew Gardens
Surrey TW9 4JF England
Phone: 44 (0)208-392-8585;
Fax: 44 (0)208-392-9876
E-mail: Bushwd@aol.com
Free postage in the UK. Europe: air mail at cost.
Please try your bookstore first.

In memory of my father,
Neil,
who, unlike me, was not afraid of
ghosts and instilled in me his love of
history and my mother,
Mary Lanigan,
for believing anything was possible.

To my husband,
Glenn Forman,
forever being my beacon in the
darkness, and our daughter,
Jade,
who even thinks headstones are
lighthouses.

CONTENTS

ACKNOWLEDGMENTS

Thanks to: Norman J. Brouwer, Herman Melville Library, South Street Seaport Museum and the South Street Seaport Gift Shop, New York City; Joanne McMahon, Parapsychology Foundation, New York City; Ken Black, Shore Village Museum, Rockland, Maine; *Lighthouse Digest* magazine, Wells, Maine; Fire Island Lighthouse Gift Shop, Kismet, New York; Tony Poldino, lighthouse keeper, Fire Island Light; Brooklyn Public Library, Research Department, Grand Army Plaza; pen pals: Walt Cushman, Carolyn Ortiz, Giselle Ruiz, Sherrie Lewis-Cato, Joyce Healy-Volpe, Arlene Miles, Hazel J. Voleck, Inspector Alan D. Zolman, and all lighthouse aficionados who have lost cameras and almost been arrested in the pursuit of lighthouse viewing; Ethan Gross; Jeff Tauscher; Elinor A. De Wire, Louisa Ruby, Maine Lighthouse Map and Guide, Freeport; Chris Woodyard, Bruce Jenvey, *Great Lakes Cruiser*, Michigan; Candace Clifford, National Park Service, Washington, D.C.; Wayne Wheeler, United States Lighthouse Society, San Francisco; Dan McGee, Presque Isle, Michigan; Anne Webster-Wallace, Seguin Island, Maine; Donna Ray Mitchell, Old Baldy Foundation, Wilmington, North Carolina; Coastal Georgia Historic Society, St. Simons Island, Georgia; Sandra Johnson, Pensacola Historical Society; Outer Banks Lighthouse Society, Nags Head, North Carolina; Jerry Biggs, Great Lakes Lighthouse Keepers Association; Jeff Gamble and Linda Gamble, Big Bay Point Lighthouse, Big Bay, Michigan; Cullen Chambers, Tybee Island Light, Georgia; Kathy Fleming and Karen Harvey, St. Augustine Light, Florida; Nadine Everette, National Trust for Historic Preservation, Washington, D.C.; Sharon Upchurch, Haig Point, South Carolina; Ted Panayotoff, The Elms B&B, Camden, Maine; Matthew Parker, Brooklyn Workstation; David Lightman, Computer Magic, Brooklyn; Sherri Linsenbach; Nina Kaufman, my attorney; Tina Skinner, my editor, and Peter Schiffer, my publisher.

Anyone with a nonfiction story can contact me through my publisher.

Many of the lights discussed in this book are listed in the National Historic Register, which guarantees protected status by the United States government and thus insures that they will never be torn down. Others are active aids to navigation, the Coast Guard still employing their beams to maintain safe maritime travel. A few of the lighthouses are private homes. Some are endangered. It is important to respect these sites. Write to your Congressperson, urging them to maintain these great architectural links to our maritime history.

INTRODUCTION

Lighthouses are natural locations to encounter ghostly experiences. The wind whistling past their great circular stone towers, the sea moss encroaching . . . lighthouses have long had a wild, romantic lore that fits well with ghost stories. Lamps have been tended, brass polished, windows cleaned, tools taken and returned, jackets thrown off hooks onto floors, all without explanation. And what of the mysterious child's cry, sad moans, footsteps on the circular wrought iron stairs...?

Ghosts customarily inhabit surroundings where their lives ended, rendering them an energy source left behind at death. A type of electric force can be detected by a sensitive person, "someone who has tuned into the frequency," as *The Ghosts of New England Lighthouses* aptly puts it. This energy materializes as a ghost or thought projection in a person's mind, much like turning on a television.[1] Parapsychologists have noted that many hauntings occur when the barometric pressure drops. This explains why so many lighthouse specters make themselves known in the midst of inclement weather.

My haunted stories begin on the Atlantic Coast of the United States, travel to the Long Island Sound, down the Outer Banks, Chesapeake Bay, Gulf Coast, and the Pacific, go upwards to the Great Lakes and Canada, and end in the Bahamas.

Many of the stories are sad tales of keepers or their family members who have died but have been unable to leave the lighthouse or keeper's quarters. Other tales are violent. I caution parents with small children to peruse the book first, so as not to scare young ones. Now it is time to settle back on a stormy night with the sea wild and the salt spray in the air and enjoy *Ghostly Beacons: Haunted Lighthouses of North America*.

Therese Lanigan-Schmidt

IGHTHOUS GHOST STORIES

CHAPTER I

NEW ENGLAND LIGHTHOUSES

Just one year ago tonight Love
I became your blushing bride
You promised I'd be happy
But no happiness I find
For tonight I am a widow
In the cottage by the sea.

(John Rogers Thomas, "The Cottage by the Sea")[2]

MAINE

BOONE (BOON) ISLAND LIGHT

Located off the coast of York on an island six miles from the coast, Boone (also spelled Boon) Island Light's tower, at 133 feet above the water, appears to rise from the sea. Originally built in 1811, it was rebuilt and the tower height raised in 1831. The present granite tower was erected in 1855, 60 feet south of the original tower. Boone island is the setting of the poem, "Watch of Boon Island" by Celia Thaxter.[3]

Contact: (603) 431-5500.

Boon Island Light, *Courtesy of Carolyn Ortiz*

Our first story has to do with cannibalism, birds, and a keeper who froze to death in Maine, the coastal state with the most lighthouses.

Boone Island, the tallest lighthouse in Maine, is considered by former keepers to be the starkest (no grass, shade, or earth), most isolated, and most exhausting post to work. It is also the least accessible.

So isolated is Boone that in 1710, when the British merchantman ship *Nottingham* was wrecked nearby, a grizzly tale ensued. Stranded for a month, a "freezing, starving crew ate Tom, the ship's carpenter," as related in Kenneth Roberts' novel, *Boon Island*.[4]

Massive seas have heaped great boulders weighing tons against the outside doors of the lighthouse. All of the outbuildings, hen houses, storage units, boardwalks, and landing areas, have been swept away numerous times in the midst of savage gales and storms. The swaying tower was often the only refuge for keepers and their families. Their sole means of communication prior to radio and telephone was carrier pigeon.

An interesting story involving birds took place at Boone Island over one hundred years ago. Around Thanksgiving, the weather prevented the keepers from rowing the nine miles to shore for supplies. No call from the lighthouse tender (the lighthouse supply boat) was forthcoming. As such, the keepers resigned themselves to a holiday dinner of potatoes and bread. However, a flock of geese crashed into the light on Thanksgiving Eve. The next day, the aroma of roast goose and gravy drifted through the lighthouse.[5]

Keepers at Boone climbed the tall tower's one hundred and thirty steps to the watch room, then a ladder to the lantern room. A few keepers have described hearing odd wailing sounds as they sat on an old stool or box on their lonely watch. These sounds may be explained by a story passed down from ages past, and well known by the local inhabitants of York Beach.

In the 1850s, a young keeper was assigned to duty at Boone Light. His new wife accompanied him. They had a good marriage, working the light together, and considered it an ongoing honeymoon.

Four months later, a brutal midwinter storm came up. When the husband went outside to lash down the island boat, he stumbled on the icy rocks and fell into the frigid seas where he drowned. The young wife had no one to call for help. She retrieved his frozen body and placed it in the base of the tower. The terrible seas pounded at the lighthouse door as the thermometer registered five degrees below zero. The sea formed a thick steam vapor around the island, reducing visibility to about ten yards.

For the next five days, the keeper's wife climbed the one hundred and thirty stairs every few hours to insure that the wicks stayed lit. After each climb, she would return to the base of the tower and sit with the frozen body of her spouse. On the fifth day, without food or water, she collapsed from exhaustion. The light died.

Local fishermen investigated and found the young girl near death, holding the hand of her frozen husband's corpse, her mind gone. She was returned to the mainland, but never recovered from her ordeal. Since then, subsequent keepers have reported strange crying sounds.

Do her mournful wails still vibrate within the long slender tower?[6]

HENDRICKS HEAD LIGHT

Located at the Sheepscot River entrance, Hendricks Head is a fixed white beacon first lit in 1829 and located 43 feet above the waterline. It is listed in the National Historic Register and is a privately owned active aid to navigation.

In the 1870s, the keeper saw a schooner hammered to bits just off the rocky shore. All hands perished, save a baby girl who was fastened between two mattresses. She floated ashore and was rescued by the keeper. The keeper and his wife later adopted the baby girl, having just buried their baby daughter a few weeks earlier. The foundling grew up and lived a normal, happy life.

The ghost who haunts this seaport area of Southport may have been the mother of the orphaned girl. She is said to be an attractive young woman in her early twenties. One night she was seen in the area. Locals spoke to her, but she was silent. The natives did not know her or how she arrived, but said she appeared to be quite genteel. Her body was discovered the following day washed up on the beach, heavy weights bound about her waist. It was thought she was a victim of suicide or foul play. Some thought she may have been murdered by rum runners. She was interred in the local cemetery.

Some say it is she that they've observed on the beach north of the lighthouse, where it is believed she drowned. Others think she could be the mother of the baby who survived the wreck, doomed to forever wander the beach in search of her lost child. Over the last sixty years, the apparition has been seen pacing the small sandy beach near the lighthouse, and footprints have been noticed. [7]

MARSHALL POINT LIGHT

The light is located at the Port Clyde Harbor entrance. Erected in 1857, Marshall Point Light is an active aid to navigation and listed in the National Historic Register.

Contact: Marshall Point Lighthouse Museum, Marshall Pt. Rd., P.O. Box 247, Port Clyde, Maine 04855. Phone: (207) 372-6450.

Marshall Point Light, *Courtesy of Walter H. Cushman*

The site of the book, *Nellie the Lighthouse Dog*, Marshall Point Light achieved passing celebrity a few years ago as the location where a wild-looking Forrest Gump (from the movie of the same name), turned around during his cross-continent run.[8]

Renowned parapsychologist Dr. Hans Holzer enjoyed one of his "favorite cases of haunting" at Marshall Point while working for the NBC television series *In Search of . . .*", (as stated in Hans Holzer's *Haunted America*, ©1993). He received a letter from Carol Olivieri Schulte in November 1974. She wrote about an incident that happened to her in the summer of 1972, in Port Clyde, formerly Herring's Gut, a small fishing village on the Maine coast.

Schulte was asleep in her parents' summer cottage in Port Clyde. Her friend's cat, who had been sleeping in a bedroom across the hall, grew fidgety, crept into Carol's room, and roused her. Carol sat up in bed and turned on the light. She beheld, standing beside her bed, a female form in a white nightgown. The figure had small shoulders and long, flowing hair. Carol could see right through her.

Shortly after, Carol had a dream contact with the same being. She was asleep in a different room when Carol saw the same young woman. The apparition materialized in the air and appeared to be smaller than life size. She had a maternal air and was accompanied by a boy of maybe three years of age, also attired in a white gown.

Carol's brother, Bob Olivieri, also had his own odd experiences in the house. One night he was sleeping and awoke to the sound of footsteps, or at least what he thought were footsteps. It sounded "like slippers or baby's feet in pajamas," he related. He peered into the hallway and as soon as he did, the sound ceased. Olivieri returned to bed and again heard footsteps. Again, as soon as he looked into the hallway, the noise stopped.

He checked the rooms where his sister and nephew were sleeping as well as his parents' room. All were asleep. Yet, he kept hearing footsteps for an hour.

Olivieri tried to lie down again. As soon as he did, the steps resumed. A few minutes passed by, and he detected a pressure on his sheets, starting from Olivieri's feet and going up, until something pulled his hair!

Plans were made to have Carol and her family join Dr. Holzer, his crew, and NBC management at the house for an inquiry and filming in May of 1976. The trance medium was Ingrid Beckman.

Holzer brought Ingrid into the house, along with his crew to record for NBC what might happen. He asked Ingrid, who knew nothing of the history of the house prior to this visit, to detail whatever psychic impressions she was gathering about the house and its people.

She related that there was a story attached to the site that took place in the 1820s or 1840s. In a trance-like state and consequently able to speak with the spirits directly, Ingrid detected a woman with a weighty feeling of sorrow. Ingrid also felt that an older building was once at the same location, an eighteenth century house, like a saltbox, situated on the water.

Ingrid felt a woman's presence with the house as well as a story connected with a man and the sea. Feeling the upstairs to be the most active area of the house, she detected a woman who watches from the windows, "waiting for somebody to come back." Ingrid received an impression that a double-masted schooner was constructed on the Kennebec River and that the woman's husband sailed on it.

Ingrid detected that the woman was throughout the house, still hoping for this man to return. She sensed a storm that the woman was quite disturbed about that occurred in the month of November.

The woman was very unhappy, Ingrid indicated, her name was Margaret and it was 1843. "Her husband went on a ship, to come back in two years." Ingrid noted. Margaret's husband's name was James and had a position on a whaling ship, the *St. Catherine* or *St. Catherines.*

There were two children, Philip, who went to sea, and Francis, who died of cholera at age seventeen.

"...[S]omething about a lighthouse disturbs her. . . She doesn't feel that it's been well kept," Ingrid stated.

"Tell her that she . . . need not stay where so much unhappiness has transpired in her life. . . . tell her to call out to her husband, James." Holzer instructed.

Ingrid, still in a trance, responded:

"They are gone," she related.

The camera crew packed up, so that they could continue shooting in the morning. But for Holzer, the real work followed, authenticating the information Ingrid had picked up. He contacted an expert who was familiar with both the area and its history, ex-sailor Commander Albert Smalley. Smalley knew that a person named Hatton lived in Port Clyde prior to 1850 and that he was a sailor. In addition, there was a ship named the *St. Catherine* in the area.

Holzer asked about the lighthouse not far from Port Clyde and Commander Smalley indicated that it was erected in 1833. He then inquired about any tales of a woman phantom in connection with the lighthouse. Smalley replied that she "used to appear, especially on foggy nights. . . something about her ringing the bell at the lighthouse."

Since the seance, nothing further has been heard from the ghostly lady of Port Clyde. It is thought she has finally been reunited with her husband, who went down in a gale over one hundred years ago.[9]

MATINICUS ROCK LIGHT (TWIN TOWERS)

The light is six miles south of Matinicus Island, 23 miles off the coast and was erected in 1827. The National Audobon Society utilizes the former keeper's quarters in the summer as part of Project Puffin, a continuing restoration project for the once-endangered species.[10]

Contact: Offshore Freight and Passenger Company, Matinicus Island, Maine 04851. (207) 336-3700 (days), (207) 366-3926 (evenings).

Matinicus Rock was one of the few remote island stations that still had families in residence. Children studied by correspondence course.

Records of destructive storms fill the pages of lighthouse logbooks. An abrupt January 27, 1839 logbook entry read: "Lighthouse tore down by the sea."[11]

Matinicus Rock is the setting for *Keep the Light Burning Abbie*, the true story of Abbie Burgess Grant. In January 1856 at the age of 14, when her father, Keeper Samuel Burgess was detained ashore by a storm, fourteen-year-old Abbie worked tirelessly to keep the lamps burning in both towers while 30-40 foot waves raged over Matinicus Rock.

As the storm intensified and the old keeper's house began to collapse, she moved her mother and sisters into the north tower, away from the brunt of the storm, wind and waves. She then hurried out to the chicken coop to rescue her pet hens. It was a wise decision, because the old house and chicken coop were washed away at the height of the storm, and the eggs produced by the hens in the days that followed were the only food the women had until Keeper Burgess could return, three weeks later.

Abbie later became assistant keeper to her husband at Matinicus, where they raised four children.

Fifty years after her death, Abbie Burgess finally got the lighthouse symbol inscribed on her tombstone, courtesy of noted maritime author Edward Rowe Snow.

Many years ago, it is said that a keeper committed suicide at Matinicus Rock. The ghost of the dead man did not rest easy, and it is probably his ghost that haunted the lighthouse until at least 1986.

At that time, part of the original dwelling was unoccupied and used as a kind of storehouse. When the older keepers were relieved by the new keepers, they neglected to tell them about the building.

When the relief crew opened the door to this part of the structure, they were immediately plagued by unexplained occurrences. Cups fell off the table, doors banged, and cupboards would not stay closed. Light bulbs burned out almost daily, and even the light itself was extinguished.

Upon closing the door, all returned to normal, until an officer came out to inspect the station. He ordered the door opened. Over the crew's misgivings, it was opened, for the officer was not one who believed in ghosts.

But before the officer left the island, lights went out, the generator quit, and cups fell off the table. The officer's last command as he left the rocks was: "Shut that damned door and keep it shut!"

The crew was happy to obey and peace has ruled Matinicus Rock since.[12]

Rev. E. S. Ufford wrote "Take Good Care of the Light" at the request of the dying keeper, dedicated to his daughter, which I quote in part:

> ". . . The rising gale has a moaning sound
> O, some gallant ship may go aground,
> Take good care of the light. . .
> A wakeful eye scans the waters o'er
> For the welcome beacon on the shore,
> My child, the tower I'll climb no more,
> Take good care of the light..."[13]

OWLS HEAD LIGHT

Located at West Penobscot Bay, Rockland Harbor, the current twenty-foot tower, perched on a rocky ledge one hundred feet above the water line, was erected in 1852. The light is listed in the National Historic Register and is an active aid to navigation. The keeper's quarters are used as Coast Guard housing. There is no admittance to the light, but viewing only.

Contact: The Rockland-Thomaston Area Chamber of Commerce, P.O. Box 508, Rockland, Maine 04841-0508. (207) 596-0376.

Owls Head Light, *Courtesy of Theodore J. Panayotoff*

The following story is dedicated to the memory of my father, who always believed in keeping the thermostat down.

As with all lighthouses, Owls Head Light at one time was cared for by a "wickie," an affectionate title bestowed on the keeper by Coast Guard employees. "Wickies" were chief petty officers who came into the Coast Guard from the old Lighthouse Service. These old salts used to care for the wicks to keep the lights shining.

Wickies told accounts of a prior keeper who passed away at the light station, "but is perhaps not so dead," as they have whispered. His spirit can be seen still maintaining the job as keeper. The old captain likes to keep the thermostat down. As such, the building's temperature is always frigid. Thermostats placed at a comfort zone are inexplicably turned down. Perhaps the explanation is that when the old captain lived there, he was on a "tight budget" and fuel conservation was essential.

The keeper's house is situated about two hundred feet down a slanting boardwalk from the precipice where the tower sits. Keepers have described footprints discovered on the walkway leading to the light. The footprints of a man's boot, about shoe size ten and a half, go up but do not come back and have been observed after snowstorms and when the boardwalk has been blanketed by heavy mist.

One keeper said that when he followed the prints, he discovered the massive steel door of the tower swinging open. This door had been locked the prior night and inspected twice for security reasons. As the keeper came into the tower, he felt as if someone was with him, breathing on his back. The keeper noticed a form out of the corner of his eye, but when he turned his head the figure vanished. An elderly man's presence has been repeatedly felt in this area.

At times, the case around the Fresnel lens was opened, and it appeared that someone attempted to light the lantern. Brass has been polished, silverware heard to rattle, glasses vibrated, and doors slammed shut, all for no apparent reason. A few keepers have observed the specter of an old man floating by the windows.

No one knows who the old captain is, "but he is content to have his presence felt, and he doesn't want to lose his job," subsequent keepers have reported.

There is also a tale of an older woman who has been spotted in the house's kitchen area. She has been given the name of "Little Lady." Her ghost is one of a caring individual with gray hair and a lovely face. When her presence is felt, a feeling of tranquillity, happiness, and well being comes over the area. Day-to-day worries seem to evaporate.

She customarily materializes when ships' clocks strike eleven.[14]

SEGUIN ISLAND LIGHT

Located two miles out to sea, Seguin Island, south of Georgetown, is the second oldest light on the Maine coast. Commissioned under George Washington, it was built in 1795 and rebuilt in 1819. It is one of the tallest, at 188 feet above sea level, and foggiest locations (2,734 hours of fog in a one-year period) of all coastal lighthouses. The light features Maine's only First Order Fresnel lens. (The Fresnel [pronounced "frenel"] lens, invented in the nineteenth century, revolutionized light keeping. The lenses ranged from the most powerful, The First Order, through the Seventh Order, the least strong. They replaced the smokey whale and other oils formerly used to keep the lights burning, bringing light keeping into the modern age with the use of diffraction.)

Contact: Friends of Seguin Island, P.O. Box 866, Bath, Maine 04530-0866. (207) 371-2508.

Seguin Island Light, *Courtesy of Carolyn Ortiz*

The following story has to do with a keeper's wife who kept playing the piano, even after her death in a murder/suicide in the mid-1800s.

Seguin Island from the air resembles a large turtle, with coves forming the feet and head, locals say. Once a wooded island, it is presently barren. "The setting is all here for a haunting," according to the pamphlet, *Ghosts on Seguin.*

The keeper's wife kept playing the same tune on the piano for hours without a break. The keeper lost his mind and destroyed the piano, his wife, and himself with his ax.

It's said she plays on, though. Passing ships report that the same monotonous piano tune can be heard carried across the waves from the lighthouse on calm nights.

Additionally, a keeper's ghost complete with slickers has been sighted climbing the stairway leading to the tower. Another time, the specter was spotted standing behind one keeper while a checker game was underway. The sound of a bouncing ball, similar to a basketball, was heard from the upstairs bedroom. Cold spots have brushed by men while they were polishing brass, and jackets have been taken off their hooks and thrown onto the floor. Tools mysteriously misplaced materialize later in the same location from where they were taken.

In the early 1970s and 1980s, a Coast Guard personnel crew inhabited the island and one mate related numerous encounters.

The specter, or "Old Captain" as he is called, makes himself right at home. He has been seen on several occasions ascending the narrow, spiral, iron stairway leading up to the tower. It is thought that the Old Captain could still be trying to service the light.

Keepers have also seen a young girl running up and down the stairs, waving at them. Some have heard her laughing. It is known that a young girl died on the island, and her parents entombed her by the generator house.

A notable part of the island is the land mass between the lighthouse and the fog horn, one of the most powerful fog horns of any coastal lighthouse. It is so powerful that its volume has knocked sea gulls out of the air. Both the Old Captain and the little girl have been spotted in this location, and there have been human-like sounds ranging from groans to laughter heard there, keepers report.

One of the more difficult lighthouses to visit, the entrance to the chief living quarters is via a trolley track ramp. A dory is pulled up to the boathouse by a motor and passengers walk up a narrow wooden walkway next to the tracks, like those by slick river beds or sides of mountains.

In 1985, as the station was readied for automation, the warrant officer in charge had an encounter with the ghost of the Old Captain. All household goods were being packed for shipment to the mainland. The work crew had finished for the night and everyone was asleep. Suddenly the officer was roused by the shaking of his bed. A ghost in oil skins stood at the end of the bed, shouting in pitiful tones: "Don't take the furniture. Please leave my house alone!"

The officer jumped out of bed and ran into the next room.

When the furniture was loaded onto the dory on the skid the next day, the officer issued orders to start up the engine and moved to lower the dory slowly down the track to the ocean two-hundred feet below.

The motor suddenly stopped, the chain holding the dory broke, and the loaded boat went down the track full speed, hit the ocean, and sank under the impact. "Furniture and all were lost," the Coast Guard later stated. The warrant officer maintains the Old Captain was involved, because this had never happened before.

Ever since he was assigned to the Group South Portland Coast Guard Station, roughly two miles south of the lighthouse, Lieutenant Peter Ganzer heard officers tell stories of doors mysteriously opening and closing, piano music playing when there was no piano, and someone coughing when all the men were in the same room and none had a cold.[15]

WOOD ISLAND LIGHT

Located at the east side of the island near Saco in Biddeford, erected in 1858, Wood Island Light is seventy one feet above the water. The light is listed in the National Historic Register and is an active aid to navigation, located in a bird sanctuary.

Wood Island Light, *Courtesy of Carolyn Ortiz*

Liquor has been the cause of more than one ghostly sighting. At Wood Island, a light on *Lighthouse Digest*'s Endangered List, alcohol figures prominently.

Wood Island has suffered through numerous gales. One of the worst in 1869 almost destroyed the island. Several of the "old salts" who know these waters well have fascinating stories to tell, and say that the island is jinxed or haunted by a voodoo spirit. From bizarre shipwrecks to murders, there is much eerie lore associated with the island.

The island's specter is said to be the ghost of a twenty-five-year-old drifter and heavy drinker.

In the late 1800s, "a powerful giant of a Biddeford Pool lobsterman," as he was known locally, constructed a shack on Wood Island, thereby setting up squatter's rights along with a liquor-loving drifter. In addition to being a lobsterman, he was also a special deputy sheriff. He was joined by the liquor-loving drifter.

One afternoon, the deputy sheriff came back from the mainland and found the young man totally inebriated and quite disorderly. The young man pointed a rifle at the deputy sheriff, who attempted to disarm him, but in so doing, the sheriff was shot dead.

The drunkard tried to turn himself in to the lighthouse keeper, but was told to go to the mainland and report the shooting to the police. Instead, "he returned to his rude shed on the west end of the island and put the rifle to his own head," it was reported.

Since this suicide/murder, a phantom has been spotted on the island and his presence felt. He seems to be friendly and plays tricks which are not malevolent. Window shades have been lowered and odd sounds heard, but the most prevailing antic is the opening and closing of doors. Locked doors are discovered open and swinging, doors left open and bolstered have slammed shut. Banging noises are also commonplace.

Former keepers have coexisted with the ghost as if he was one of the crew. "Can you imagine approaching a door, the latch turning, and the door opening as you enter, all on its own?" one keeper remarked. The ghost apparently is observing the comings and goings in the lighthouse, always ready to be of service.

If you were a keeper on the island, you might well think that many of the spirits from the past remain behind.[16]

NEW HAMPSHIRE

ISLE OF SHOALS (WHITE ISLAND) LIGHT

Located at the Piscataqua River Entrance, six miles off the coast southeast of Portsmouth, the White Island Light was rebuilt in 1859. The light is fifty-eight feet high and located eighteen feet from the first lighthouse. The Isle of Shoals (White Island) Light is listed in the National Historic Register, is an active aid to navigation, and is an artists' retreat in a state park.

Contact: Isles of Shoals Steamship Company, Box 311, Portsmouth, New Hampshire 03802-0311. Phone: (603) 431-5500.

Liquor, Captain Kidd, and Blackbeard play an important part in our next tale, a rather gory one.

Seven small islands comprise the Isles of Shoals: Duck, Appledore, Smuttynose, and Cedar are within the State of Maine; Star, Londoner's, and White pay taxes to New Hampshire. The name "Isles of Shoals" comes from the "shoaling" or "schooling" of exceptionally large numbers of fish in their waters.[17]

Of the Shoals, Appledore, Star, and Smuttynose are the most widely known islands. They were first mapped and charted in 1614 by the English explorer Captain John Smith. According to the Kittery (Maine) Historical Society, they were occupied by, "[A] motley company of fisherman, pirates, and seal hunters, who lived there in great uproar and content."

The Georgeana General Court thought the situation might be greatly improved if they revoked a decree that disallowed women on the islands, saying, "As the fishermen of the Isle of Shoals will entertain womanhood, they have liberty to sit down there, provided they shall not sell either wine beare or liquor."[18]

By the mid-nineteenth century, tourists and summer folks discovered the Shoals during the warm months.

There are many ghost stories in the Shoals, including tales involving the pirates Captain Kidd and Blackbeard, a butcher, the "pirate bride," and "the lady in white."

Philip Babb was an early settler and constable for the islands. Babb operated a tavern and a butcher shop on Appledore and butchered hogs near a cove that came to be named for him. He died a wealthy man in 1671.

According to the island's most acclaimed historian, Celia Thaxter, Babb was an extremely evil man for whom there was, even after death, no peace. He was said to have been one of Captain Kidd's men, and it was staunchly regarded by the islanders that his specter haunted the cove bearing his name. Nathaniel Hawthorne wrote of the ghost, describing Babb's "luminous appearance about him as he walks, and his face . . . pale and very dreadful."[19]

A tale is told that one night an islander was at his workshop when he saw a deranged man racing in his direction. The man's spectral face had the sunken eyes of a corpse, but the islander thought it was just a friend trying to pull his leg. The diabolical figure yanked a long, sharp knife from its belt and brandished it in the islander's face. The Shoaler bolted, howling all the way home, where he discovered the friend he had thought was pulling his leg eating his supper.

Another time, an islander was sitting on the porch of his home one spring night looking toward Babb's Cove. He beheld a form which made its way toward a path to the islander's house. The islander had not heard footsteps on the stony beach and got up from his chair to "intercept the mysterious form," according to *Haunted New England*.

As the form grew closer, the Shoaler was terrified "to see the vacant eyes and glowing frock of Babb's ghost." The Shoaler cried out, inquiring what the ghost wished. Babb continued to come forward, "his figure waxing and waning in distinction" until he vanished.

One of the most sentimental ghost stories of the Isle of Shoals is that of the pirate bride. The Shoals have quite an extensive history of being inhabited by pirates. "It was said that the Shoalers welcomed them as friends," according to *Maine Ghosts & Legends*. These scoundrels hid out in the Shoals where they buried their stolen treasure.

A compatriot of the bloodthirsty Edward "Blackbeard" Teach, a pirate named Scot, was said to have hidden an immense treasure on Appledore. When he departed for his next pirating voyage, he forced his young bride to vow that she would remain behind on the island to protect his booty. But the pirate never returned.

Two hundred years later, a man ambling about the cliffs at Appledore, gazing at the sea, felt there was a person standing near him. "He turned to see a beautiful young woman . . .," wrote Celia Thaxter in *Among the Isles of Shoals*. The woman, too, was gazing out at the sea, but with a yearning that took the vacationer by surprise. He surmised that she was the wife of a fisherman and asked if there was any sign of her fisherman husband. She turned and looked at him, and said simply, "He will come again." She then faded behind a large rock and left the man standing alone.

The man told many Shoalers about the woman, but none knew of her. He decided to revisit the same area the next day. After a rough crossing, he made his way to the cliffs. He climbed over the rocks and reached the forsaken precipice where he first beheld the young woman. She was not there, but through the wind and rain he made out her melancholy voice repeating: "He will come again."

A peculiar feeling of peace permeated the air the last time he observed the ghost bride at twilight. He positioned himself on the cliff and anticipated her appearance, which was imminent. This time, however, her previously cold, vacant eyes had become soft and warm. The man was so unnerved and scared by this alteration that, as a result, he never returned.

What of the pirate bride? Thaxter speculates that "[I]t is she . . . who laments like a Banshee before the tempests, wailing through the gorges at Appledore." Thaxter wrote that this ghost scares picnickers on Duck Island, materializing sometimes as a young girl.

A variation of that story takes places just east of the lighthouse on the islands of Smuttynose and Star. A "lady in white" is said to ramble there, one of the wives of the notorious pirate Blackbeard, who is thought to have buried treasure here. The story goes that he was almost captured and had to make a quick getaway and left his lady in white behind. Locals have stated that her wails, "He shall return," can still be made out "on a cold, crisp evening."

An account of the pirate bride by an unknown writer appeared in an 1826 newspaper from a nearby mainland city. As the writer stood on a long, low point of Appledore Island, he grew conscious of a woman standing near him, "fair as a lily and as still. She stood with her eyes fixed on the far distance, without motion, without sound." He thought her to be the wife "or lover of a fisherman."

"She turned instantly," he wrote, "and fixing me with the most melancholy blue eyes I ever beheld, said quietly: 'He will come again.' With that, she vanished silently around a jutting rock.."

Afterwards, the writer came back often to that same location. He often found the wraith standing beside him, "silent as when I first saw her, except to say: 'He will come again,' and these words came upon the mind rather than upon the ear. . . . I observed that shells were never crushed beneath her footsteps, nor did her garments rustle. When the winds were so furious that I could scarcely stand in their sweep, the light hair lay upon her forehead without lifting a fibre."

It is thought that the maiden still waits, forever obedient to her pledge.[20]

The Isles of Shoals are empty save for a few private summer homes. A marine laboratory and a religious conference center, used mostly in the warmer months, are the only remnants of civilization left on Appledore. Therefore, if the pirate bride remains there, she has the whole island to herself now, uttering the sad lamentation: "He will come again."[21]

RHODE ISLAND

BLOCK ISLAND (SOUTHEAST) LIGHT

Located at Mohegan Bluffs, two hundred feet above sea level, Block Island (Southeast) light is the tallest light in New England. It features an octagonal brick tower that was constructed in 1875. The light is listed in the National Historic Register, and flashes green, unusual for a New England Lighthouse.

Contact: Block Island (Southeast) Lighthouse Foundation, P.O. Box 949, Block Island, Rhode Island 02807. (401) 466-5009.

Block Island (Southeast) Light, *Courtesy of Giselle Ruiz*

President and Hillary Clinton toured Block Island (Southeast) Lighthouse in August, 1997. They climbed to the top of the tower and waved to the crowd below. Clinton was the third president to visit the lighthouse, following presidents Dwight Eisenhower in 1958 and Ulysses S. Grant in 1875.

The light is located on historic land. The Mohegan Indians from eastern Long Island were driven there and starved by the Manisses Indians many years before the English colonized the island.

In the early 1900s, a keeper hated his wife. He hurled her to her death off the round staircase immediately beneath the pedestal where the flashing light sits, according to *The Ghosts of New England Lighthouses.*

A woman's ghost now walks the house. She does not annoy women, but delights in bothering men. Among other antics, she has chased them out of rooms, locked them out of the house, and lifted and jarred their beds. She also fancies slamming doors and throwing things at some of the male keepers.

Cold spots have been felt in several sections of the house, usually an indication of a ghost. "The rest of the room may be a high temperature, but this one area will always remain chilly," a keeper stated.

One keeper was beleaguered repeatedly. It became so intolerable that one night, "he was chased out of his bedroom and through the house." He ran from the house as she slammed the door and locked him out, "dressed only in his underwear."

Another activity of the ghost is the constant rearrangement of furniture and artifacts. Keepers have come back to their bedrooms to discover the room turned around. The bed has been relocated, chairs pushed to new areas, and all bureau pictures turned upside down. Many keepers have returned to discover their clothes, formerly hanging in the closet, now lying on the bed. "Bureau drawers have been opened during the night and socks flung around the room," keepers reported.

The specter has been witnessed traveling so quickly up and down the stairs that many keepers have squeezed their bodies against the wall to allow her to pass as she flies by. The kitchen seems to be one of her preferred rooms. "Food has been thrown across the room, dishes have been smashed for no reason, . . . and one keeper reports that he would find the stove burner under his pots and pans turned up to full blast. He would be cooking on medium to low heat, would leave for just a few seconds and return to burned food,"

In its constant battle with the deteriorating bluffs and encroaching sea, the Block Island (Southeast) Light was moved back two hundred and fifty feet from its original location in 1993. Oftentimes when a haunted building is moved, the entity will drift away. We shall see if this is the case with the Block Island (Southeast) Light.[22]

MASSACHUSETTS

PLYMOUTH (GURNET) LIGHT STATION

Originally twin beacons established in 1769, the present Plymouth (Gurnet) Light Station, dating from 1843, is the oldest wooden lighthouse in the United States. Moved in 1998, the light is located at the end of Gurnet Point, 3.8 nautical miles northeast of Plymouth Rock. Situated within Fort Andrews, a Revolutionary War fort where a British frigate ran aground north of the light, historian Edward Rowe Snow asserts that the light was hit by a cannon ball during the ensuing battle. There is no admittance but viewing only.[23]

Contact: Bill and Debbi Ricci, P.O. Box 2119, Duxbury, Massachusetts 02331.

Plymouth (Gurnet) Light, *Courtesy of Carolyn Ortiz*

Plymouth settlement's first beacon was built on John and Hannah Thomas' property in 1769, at the end of land pilgrims named the Gurnet, in commemoration of a fish abundant in the waters of their European homeland. The colony's agreement with John and Hannah was typical for that era. Instead of the land being bought, John Thomas allowed the lighthouse to be built on his property so long as his family was allowed to tend it.

Plymouth's twenty-foot tower was constructed as twin lights with two separate towers, two lanterns, and twice the usual work for the keeper.

The first official lady lightkeeper on record in the United States was Hannah Thomas of Plymouth. Mrs. Thomas assisted her husband at first and shouldered full charge after his death. She executed the same duties as her male counterparts in addition to keeping her home and raising a family. In 1790, when the lighthouse was ceded to the federal government, Mrs. Thomas was still the official keeper and tended it for two decades.[24]

Bob Shanklin and his wife, Sandra, were hired to take at-dawn pictures of the Gurnet Light in the 1990s. Shanklin awoke in the night and suddenly saw a lady materialize whom he described as having the saddest eyes he'd ever seen. She stood by where Sandra was sleeping.[25]

Shanklin believes Hannah Thomas is the sad-eyed lady, unable to leave the light she spent most of her life at?

MINOTS LEDGE LIGHT

First illuminated on September 10, 1826, the second Minots Ledge Light was constructed in 1860. A twenty-foot tower on a ledge one hundred feet above the water, Minots Ledge Light was the first U.S. lighthouse to be built directly exposed to the open ocean. It is listed in the National Historic Register and is an active aid to navigation.

Contact: Lightkeepers Corporation, P.O. Box 514, Cohasset, Massachusetts 02025. (617) 383-0505.

Minots Ledge Light may truly be one of the most celebrated in verse of all the haunted lighthouses, as evidenced by this excerpted poem from *Harper's New Monthly Magazine* of April 1861:

> "Like spectral hounds across the sky
> The white clouds scud before the storm
> And naked in the howling night
> The red-eyed lighthouse lifts its form. . .
> The white spray beats against the panes
> Like some wet ghost that down the air
> Is hunted by a troop of fiends,
> And seeks a shelter any where."
>
> (FitzJames O'Brien, "Minot's Ledge")[26]

Regarded as the most treacherous light on the coast of New England, the original tower was built to guide vessels away from the Cohasset Reefs. The reefs are a sequence of perilous rocks immersed under the rolling tides that posed immense navigational dangers to ships voyaging off the coast of Cape Cod.

Native tribes have their own theory as to what is behind the danger of the reefs: "Hobomock, the Evil One according to the local Native Americans, lived under the ledges off the shores of Cohasset. . . In his fury, he created the wild northeast gales that churn the seas into a dreaded maelstrom. To placate him, Native Americans left gifts on the rocks."[27]

On April 14, 1851, a powerful nor'easter gathered strength. On duty were two assistant keepers, Joseph Antoine and Joseph Wilson. By the evening of the 16th, the platform or base of the lighthouse was washed ashore.

Wilson dashed off a fast note, that read: "Wednesday night, April 16. The lighthouse won't stand over tonight, she shakes 2 feet each way now. . . JW & JA." [initials of doomed lightkeepers][28]

At nightfall, the light could still be seen burning until 10:00 P.M. when it was finally lost from sight. In the early morning of April 17th, when the "streaming tide and the in-rushing hurricane met at Minots," as was later reported, a furious striking of the lighthouse bell was heard. It has been said that moments prior to the original tower falling into the sea, the doomed keepers "took a sledge hammer and pounded on the bell," saying farewell to their loved ones on shore.

Up to the last, the assistant keepers on the tower maintained the light, "face-to-face with death for the honor of the lighthouse service." One was German or Dutch; the other Portuguese. The remains of these keepers were washed ashore on Gull Island and recovered the following day.

"The mad waves leaped and tumbled wildly and in seeming exultation over its site," *The Boston Daily Journal* reported in April, 1851.[29]

"When it [the hurricane] lifted, naught was seen over Minots Ledge but the sea, its white crest streaming triumphantly in the gale," the pa-

Minots Ledge Light, *Courtesy of Carolyn Ortiz*

pers reported. There was never a monument raised for these brave men, but it is thought that their ghosts haunt Minots Ledge.

Following the destruction of the first lighthouse, Congress made an allocation for the building of another, which was finished in September 1860 at a cost of $300,000. One of the most striking wave-swept lighthouses of the world, the Lighthouse Board describes it as an "engineering work of first rank, . . . situated one mile offshore, six miles southeasterly of Boston entrance on a dangerous reef which is awash at low water." The lighthouse took five years to complete and lodging is for keepers only. Families are housed at Cohasset.

Keepers of the tower have stated that those who drowned with the old lighthouse, among others, haunt the new tower. Odd sounds have been heard in the oil room, the clanking of cans and clinking of glass, "as if someone were at work there." Baffling tales are told of maps being filed and the lens and lantern being cleaned.

For many years, mariners who sailed by Minots have asserted that they hear odd voices, "and see ghostlike fixtures clinging to the lower section of the ladder." It is said that the Portuguese fishermen, who had taken their compatriot, Joseph Antoine to serve his turn as assistant keeper, saw the specter many times thereafter. Former keeper Fitzpatrick stated that many Portuguese fishermen to this day still do not venture near the tower.

The specter of young Antoine has routinely been spotted and heard just before nor'easters. The ghost apparently puts in a showing to alert his countrymen of impending danger. Some sailors say that they have seen his ghost clutching the lower rungs of the lighthouse ladder, "with the gathering surf sweeping over him as he cries out, 'Keep away, keep away!' "[30]

Another tale involves work at the tower. After the Civil War, the head keeper realized that the lamp and the lens had been radiantly polished that morning, although the assistant keeper, whose assignment it was to shine it, was fast asleep. A week later, the assistant keeper noted that the same procedure had been duplicated, although neither man had done it. The ghosts of the two keepers who perished in 1851 received full recognition for the polishing work..[31]

In the old tower, when a watch was finished, the keeper in the watch room summoned his replacement by banging on a pipe, which ran up from the lower room. The other keeper would rap in response to inform the watch that he had heard the signal and would be up immediately. In the new tower, the watch is designated and answer given by electric bells.

One night, as the midnight watch was coming to a close, a keeper in the new tower was on watch and inadvertently bent forward and rapped on the pipe. A few minutes later, he was alarmed to hear a rap in reply from below. The keeper waited for his replacement, but in vain. He pressed the button of the electric bells, and after the usual pause, the bell in the watch room rang the answer from below. The man on watch could hear footsteps on the iron stairs below. He had not heard the rapping and so made no answer. His first clue of the change of watch had been the ringing of the bell.

The Coast Guard automated the tower in 1947, and there are plans underway to honor the drowned keepers. The town of Cohasset has formally voted to allow a granite memorial to be placed on Government Island. The proposed memorial will be a half-ton stone of polished black granite bearing a carving of the lighthouse and a brief record of the Keepers' deed. At the bottom will be the old motto: "They kept the good light."

The monument will be placed between the twenty-six-foot replica of the top of the Minots Light tower and the templates where the granite blocks for the lighthouse were shaped in 1855.[32]

Numerous fierce storms have battered Minots Ledge since those two brave men died. On several of these nights, keepers have seen this code." The light beacon blinks, 1-4-3. With the passage of time, the 1-4-3 blinking became regarded as the "I Love You" light. Locals reminisce about time spent on the beach with the ones they love at night and "spooning" to the I Love You Light.[33]

It is interesting that the feeling for this light that is so haunted is also one of romance. The sequence "1-4-3" has been engraved inside wedding bands, to forever seal the love that people have found in the shadow of the haunted Minots Ledge Light.[34]

CHAPTER II

NORTHEAST LIGHTHOUSES

CONNECTICUT

NEW LONDON LEDGE LIGHT

Located at the mouth of New London Harbor, one mile offshore, on a wave-swept site, the New London Ledge Light was erected in 1909 and automated in 1986. Listed in the National Historic Register, the light is an active aid to navigation. There is no admittance to the light, but viewing only.

Contact: New London Ledge Lighthouse Foundation, P.O. Box 855, New London, Connecticut 06320. (203) 442-2222.

New London Ledge Light, *Courtesy of Walter H. Cushman*

New London Ledge Light actually has a pet name for its resident ghost, "Ernie," the spirit of a rejected husband.

An uncommon example of a joined light tower and keeper's dwelling constructed in a revival style (a design popular under the Lighthouse Board from 1852-1920), the New London Ledge Light in 1936 was run privately by one family before the 1939 Coast Guard takeover.

A keeper, Ernie, learned that his wife had run off with a Block Island ferry boat captain. Ernie was so distressed that he climbed to the top of the tower and leaped from the catwalk surrounding the lantern gallery, "dashing to his death," according to *Lights and Legends*.

Another variation of how Ernie came to an end was that, after discovering his wife had run off, he slashed his throat and hurled himself off the upper level of the lighthouse, leaving a trail of blood down the outside of the building. His body was never discovered.

Subsequent keepers say that the massive curved door to the lighthouse, which is locked from the inside, sometimes opens without explanation. "The wind can be blamed for many of the strange noises we hear, but I know the sound of that door opening up and no wind ever did that," a Coast Guardsman said.

Many Coast Guardsmen assigned to the light have heard the decks being swabbed in the early morning hours. Others have made out footfalls or felt cold spots in the lighthouse rooms. Ernie materializes at the top of the stairs for a few seconds, then disappears. Scraping noises, bumps, and soft footfalls are all said to emanate from Ernie, and he is accused of the random, surprising, switching on and off of the light signal and the fog horn. "None of the electronic devices the Coast Guard has added to the lighthouse have been able to detect Ernie's tortured ghost opening the catwalk door or swabbing the decks in the dead of night," it has been reported.[35]

A lighthouse keeper, identified only as David, told psychic investigators who performed a 1981 seance at the lighthouse, that: "We found paint cans opened up downstairs with paintbrushes in them. Lights would go on and off . . . coffee cups move on the table and the refrigerator door opens and closes. I've heard him walking upstairs when both of us [two men are on duty at the light at a time] were downstairs. Doors would open and close. The TV has gone off on me."

At the time of the seance, Chief Lighthouse Keeper John Etheridge spoke of an old radio in Ernie's former room. "If you moved that radio, [s]omething would move it back." A genuine specter, Etheridge reports, has materialized only in front of women and children.

A woman who dwelled in the lighthouse with her children related how she was roused by something at the end of her bed at night. She said that it was a man, approximately six-feet, one-inch tall, "slender, bearded, wearing a rain hat and a slicker." Her children were also stirred by a similar form. Etheridge said Randy, a lighthouse keeper, described how he would descend the ladder and could make out someone "calling his name."

One of the most oft-told Ernie tales is of "the doubting fishermen." Etheridge tells the story thus: "There were some fishermen who came out to visit the lighthouse keepers. They said they didn't believe in Ernie the ghost. Ernie doesn't like to be spoken against. When they went to get into their boat, it was adrift away from the lighthouse. . . . And these are fishermen who have been tying up boats all their lives."

In December 1981, Connecticut psychic Roger Pile was invited to come to New London Ledge Light to investigate Ernie. Pile's wife, Nancy, was to serve as the trance medium. Pile was solicited by a marine biologist, who worked with the Coast Guard and knew the light. The biologist, his wife, and the two keepers on duty, John Etheridge and David, were also present. Psychic Pile deems his ghost work as "rescues" as opposed to "exorcisms" and tapes the majority of these operations.

Ernie entered through the entranced Nancy Pile, it was later reported. He said his correct name was John Randolph. Pile inquired of Randolph if he wanted to be "helped over." Randolph said he did and spoke through the medium:

"[W]e had quarreled. She found solace with another and left . . . the fault was mine . . . I decided that my method of death would . . . be more apropos to the crime of having said too much. I took my knife, placed it to my throat, and plunged it in. . . . Imagine my surprise to find that I remained. . . . So I have stayed at the light, and I've made myself known and have enjoyed the companionship of the others."

Pile then urged the ghost to "Feel the warmth envelope you. Notice off to your right there are two pinpoints of light coming toward you, to help you across. It will be a very joyful, beautiful experience for you."

Randolph stated that he would follow the lights. Pile responded, "Go in joy and love and peace."

"Since we did the rescue," Pile reported, "it has been very quiet out there, except for one instance when it is believed that Ernie returned very briefly."

Roger Pile claims that the light is now free of Randolph, and can show affidavits from recent keepers swearing to that. A story in the June 28, 1983, *New Haven (Connecticut) Register* summed it up: "I guess Ernie is gone," stated Coast Guard Commodore Edward Wiegand, with a hint of pleasure. A few of the men based there, bored with their duty, "have missed Ernie," he added.[36]

PENFIELD REEF LIGHT

Located one mile south of Fairfield at the entrance of Black Rock Harbor, Penfield Reef Light was constructed in 1874 and automated in 1971. Listed in the National Historic Register, it is an active aid to navigation and flashes red.

Visible from both sea and shore, Penfield Reef Light embodies one of the most common, masonry dwelling with tower designs used by the Lighthouse Board in the 1860s and 1870s. A photograph of the light was included in the Lighthouse Board's exhibit at the Philadelphia 1876 Centennial Exhibition.

In all the Long Island Sound, there is no more infamous locality than Penfield Bar and Reef. During low tide, you can amble along the bar and reef just above the lighthouse, but care has to be taken. Natives speak of a family of seven who were caught "by the incoming tide on a high part of the reef and never seen again." During a November 1916 gale, nine barges from New York's Blue Line crashed into a part of Penfield Reef. As a result, Penfield Bar and Reef earned the nickname, "The Blue Line graveyard."

It is with "The Legend of Christmas Eve" that we are most concerned.

On Christmas Eve 1916, keeper Fred Jordan set out in a rowboat for shore leave while a wild gale was in full fury. Jordan's flimsy craft capsized and he drowned.

A subsequent keeper tells of seeing the form of a man attired in white "steal out of one of the rooms of the light, glide down the stairway of the tower, and disappear into the darkness outside." Downstairs, an old lighthouse journal was found on a table, opened to the page where mention of Jordan's passing was noted. The book hadn't been removed from the shelf for a long time previously. How could the journal not only make it off the shelf but be opened and turned to the entry on Jordan?

Additionally, "that lighthouse log is found open to the page for Christmas Eve 1916."

Captain R. Itten, head keeper, related a story to *The Bridgeport Sunday Post* in the 1920s "about an old saying that what the reef takes, the reef gives back." Jordan's body was found soon after his drowning. In his coat pocket was a memo to Itten, which Jordan neglected to leave behind before he "started out on his fatal ride on that rough sea." The memo advised Itten to be sure to finish the records of that morning, the same day Jordan perished, "as they had not been brought up to date."

On stormy nights, the ghost is "said to poise on the rail of the gallery that surrounds the lantern, swaying, as if in agony, or to flit among the black jagged rocks that surround the base of the light," according to *Lights and Legends*.

Recently, a yacht in distress was said to have been guided through the breakers to safety by a odd man who quickly emerged amid the surf in a rowboat. It was said that he delivered the yacht into quiet waters with great expertise. Afterward, he returned to his boat and vanished.

Many years ago, two boys fishing near the pier from a canoe were catapulted into the sea when their craft capsized. Drowning seemed imminent. A man rose from out of the rocks and hauled the boys to safety at the base of the light. They wished to thank the man, whom they assumed was one of the keepers, but he was not to be found.[37]

Could Keeper Jordan still be trying to fulfill his duties, even after his death?

NEW YORK

EXECUTION ROCKS LIGHT

Located at Sands Point, constructed in 1850 and rebuilt in 1868, Execution Rocks Light is situated atop a stone tower, fifty-four feet high. It was automated in 1979. The most powerful light on the western end of Long Island Sound, it is listed in the National Historic Register and is an active aid to navigation.

Execution Rocks Light, *Courtesy of Carolyn Ortiz*

Many say that the Execution Rocks Light is set upon the "bones of the real Patriots of the Revolution."

In the beginning of the eighteenth century, the British Colonial administration was often humiliated at public executions. Those sentenced to die, when at the gallows or in front of a firing squad, sometimes yelled out in explosive and defiant disobedience to the king. Afraid of insurrection, it was considered wise to carry out executions of colonials in private. As such, "Soldiers dug a prison deep into the rock reef at Cow Neck (Manhasset Neck) and, at low tide on execution day, a prison boat carried the condemned from Sands Point to the reef," according to *Lights and Legends*.

The condemned were manacled to huge rings placed in the walls of the pit and they drowned as the high tide slowly filled the pit and finally swept over the rocks. *Lights and Legends* states that the dead were either left and "became skeletons to drive new batches of the condemned insane before they drowned," or were hauled away and interred in unmarked graves when "the rings to which they were chained were needed for still more executions."

Although Execution Pit was off limits to the general population, its atrocity became well known in Colonial America. Many historians speculate that the actions at Execution Pit were the driving force for the line in the Declaration of Independence: "The murder they commit on the inhabitants of these United States."

When Execution Rocks Lighthouse was constructed, evidence of the savage history of Execution Rocks "burned itself into the nation's consciousness." As a result, the government set down unusual conditions for its operation. Congress mandated that never again would any person feel "chained" to Execution Rocks. Instead of mandating a set period of service for lighthouse keepers, the "keepers served as they were willing." If keepers wished to change position, they could ask for and receive an immediate "honorable" transfer "without prejudice."

It has long been said that the spirits of those convicted to perish "in the creeping horrors of a slowly rising tide" ultimately garnered their vengeance on the king's men. As George Washington and his threadbare army withdrew from Manhattan toward White Plains, a shipload of British soldiers in chase capsized on Execution Rocks, drowning all aboard.[38]

When asked if the lighthouse was haunted in a recent issue of *Lighthouse Digest*, Sam, who was responsible for the overall operation of the lighthouse, replied: "Once in a while Humphrey (the name the men gave the ghost) lets us know he's still around by rumbling through the lighthouse."[39]

Could "Humphrey" be one of the ghosts of Execution Rocks who exacted his revenge on the British troops in chase after Washington's men?

FIRE ISLAND LIGHT

Located on the south side of Long Island, the second Fire Island Light was constructed in 1858. The tower is 168 feet high and is visible twenty-one miles out to sea. An active aid to navigation in a national park, the light is listed in the National Historic Register.

Contact: Irene Rosen, Fire Island National Seashore, 120 Laurel Street, Patchogue, New York 11772. (516) 661-4876.

Fire Island Light, *Courtesy of Carolyn Ortiz*

For many immigrants, the first glimpse they had of America was not of the Statue of Liberty but the Fire Island Light.[40]

The haunting of the Fire Island Light involves not only a ghostly keeper who hung himself, but also one who still waits for a doctor who did not come in time.

Tour groups have heard old fashioned music coming from the tower, and guides have reported the sound of footsteps on the spiral stairs during bad weather. One tour guide reports that a tightly locked door to the tower was found unlocked. A keeper was said to have hung himself at the top of the tower, perhaps why a subsequent keeper would not step into the tower.

In order for him to complete his job, his wife and child had to hoist him up to the top of the tower so that he could check the light from the outside.

When the new lighthouse was being built in 1858, Lieutenant J. T. Morton was project supervisor. The Lighthouse Board's orders were to maintain the original tower and keeper's house until the new lighthouse was completed. The keeper was Nathenial Smith.

In August of that year, Morton was building the foundation of the keeper's new house, but was running out of rocks. Instead of bringing more rocks over by boat from the mainland, thus delaying the completion date, Morton decided to "recycle" rocks from the original tower and dwelling. He wanted to move the keeper and his family into a wood frame house so they could use the stones from their old home.

Keeper Smith and his family, however, preferred living in the stone house, which was made tight against the elements. Smith pleaded with Morton to allow his family to remain in their old stone house, thinking especially of his young daughter, born with a weakness of the lungs.

Morton, however, was determined to complete his project on time. He wrote a letter to Captain William Franklin, then Secretary of the Lighthouse Board, imploring him to take action against Keeper Smith's failure to follow orders. The Board immediately sent word for Smith and his family to vacate the premises at once. Smith moved his family and their belongings to the shanty that Morton proclaimed "tight" against the elements. The project was completed on time in November of 1858.

But Morton could not have anticipated the damp weather that fall. Not being as warm as the old stone house, the winds and dampness seeped right into the shanty. As a result, Keeper Smith's family was never warm in their perpetually damp quarters. His young child became quite ill and did not respond to the various medicines that had always worked before.

In December, tremendous gale force winds and snows lashed the island. Smith's child was gravely ill and running a high fever. The keeper sent word to the mainland for the doctor to come.

For three days and nights, Keeper Smith climbed the iron spiral steps to the top of the lighthouse, making sure the light was free of snow, peering out the window for the doctor, praying for him to make speed. For three days, he and his wife tended to their sick child. But the doctor didn't make it in time. Their young daughter died. Smith and his wife cremated her in the fireplace urn.

During inclement weather, tour guides have often heard "something like a man's moan." When they clean the intermittent falling plaster dust on the spiral stairs that lead into the tower, they have heard footsteps, but they never see a soul.

There are those who say Keeper Smith never really left the lighthouse, that he walks still, tending the light, climbing the iron spiral steps, still waiting for the doctor who was not to come in time.[41]

THE STATUE OF LIBERTY

The first electrically lit lighthouse in the United States, the Statue of Liberty was completed in 1886 and served as a light beacon for seventeen years.

Contact: The Statue of Liberty Monument, National Park Service, Liberty Island, New York 12754. (212) 732-1286.

Statue of Liberty, *Courtesy of Giselle Ruiz*

Before the erection of the statue, there stood on the island a star-shaped military installation called Ft. Wood. The pedestal of the statue rises above the filled in walls of the old fort on what was originally called Bedloe's Island.

The ghosts of Bedloe's Island that are said to roam these walls include the notorious pirate, Captain Kidd. Kidd lived in New York City for years and even had a reserved pew at Trinity Church before being apprehended. He was "hung out to dry," a practice where captured pirates were encased in metal clamps and hung up at the mouth of the harbor to warn other pirates that a similar fate awaited them if they did not change their evil ways. Kidd eventually died from madness and the effects of heat and starvation.

In 1825, Sergeant Gibbs was assigned to Ft. Wood along with a recruit named Carpenter. They learned that some of Kidd's treasure was secreted about the harbor by a psychic, who told them to look for a large, flat rock, wait for a full moon, and use a divining rod.

One such night, the soldiers left their barracks and found the largest, flattest rock on the island. Gibbs walked upon the beach of Bedloe's Island, divining rod in hand. The rod dipped. The treasure was beneath his feet.

Gibbs and Carpenter dug into the sand and stone. Five feet under, their shovel clanked on something solid. It was a treasure chest!

As they prepared to bring it up, they were shaken by a brilliant flash, a powerful pressure, and a frightening figure. It was the ghost of a dead pirate.

Legend has it that pirate captains always killed a crewman and dumped their lifeless body atop their buried treasure, to insure that their ghost would forever protect the treasure.

Gibbs and Carpenter's screams attracted the attention of the sentries who found them by the chest. Because Gibbs and Carpenter were beyond the walls of the Fort without permission, they were turned over to the sergeant-at-arms. They told him the story of the specter. Their descriptions differed, but both swore they would sign an affidavit that they had, indeed, seen the ghostly pirate who was forever protecting Captain Kidd's buried treasure.[42]

CHAPTER III

SOUTHERN LIGHTHOUSES

DELAWARE

LEGEND OF THE "CORPSE LIGHT

In Cape Henlopen State Park a story is often told of "the Corpse Light," not a lighthouse in the sense that we know it.

According to *The National Directory of Haunted Places*, a "cylindrical shaft or ruff stone rises out of the mist and shines a flickering beacon at ships approaching the coast." Natives call it "the Corpse Light," others "the Bad Weather Witch." The phenomena is often perceived as a lighthouse beam, and has lured many an unfortunate seaman to death.

Hundreds have died in wrecks here. The first tragedy took place on December 25, 1655. The captain of the *Devonshireman* navigated his ship directly toward the "lighthouse" during a gale. Almost two hundred people perished when the ship crashed against the rocks. On May 25, 1798, the British sloop *Debraak* was lured too close to shore and broke apart in the bay.

Legend has it that the phantom lighthouse is an old Delaware Indian curse of a "drum of stone signaling death" to all white men. The curse was placed after British soldiers murdered a gathering of Native Americans honoring a marriage service.

A phantom ship returns to replay the disaster. The specter of a single Native American atop a mysterious rock was observed by many onlookers in 1800 just prior to an excursion barge being smashed against the rocks, killing scores. As recently as 1980, the USS *Poet*, a twelve thousand-ton grain carrier, disappeared without a trace near the coast here.[43]

MARYLAND

POINT LOOKOUT LIGHT (OLD)

Located at the entrance to the Potomac River on the Chesapeake Bay in Point Lookout State Park, the old Point Lookout Light was constructed in 1830 and is a Naval Air test center. There is no admittance, but the light is visible through a fence during park hours.
Contact: (301) 872-5688.

Point Lookout is probably the most haunted lighthouse in my collection. Point Lookout's hauntings seem to stem primarily from the fact that the site on which it was built was a prisoner-of-war camp during the Civil War.

Point Lookout State Park, in southern Maryland, is a favored destination for sightseers. During the Civil War, however, it was a setting of absolute inhumanity. There are those who maintain that "faint traces of this horror still linger," according to *Guardians of the Lights*. The site was employed by the government for prisoners of war, called Camp Hoffman.

The camp never had any barracks, instead the captives were held in small tents. The lowland area was marshy and extremely detrimental to the prisoners' health. Flare-ups of smallpox, dysentery, scurvy, and other afflictions were commonplace. Between July 1863 and June 1865, over 50,000 Confederate soldiers passed through the camp. Roughly 4,000 soldiers perished there. Many years later, monuments to the Confederate deceased were constructed.

In 1964, the site was acquired by the State of Maryland for a recreational area. At that time, stories "of strange and ghostly sounds began to circulate." During the 1970s, Park Manager Gerald Sword resided in a large dwelling on the park land named "the Lighthouse." Sword maintained vehemently that the house was haunted:

"Doors opened and shut mysteriously; footsteps were heard in empty rooms and on deserted staircases. The sound of objects crashing to the ground would send people running to see what had happened. But nothing could be found," he said.

Sword heard indistinct conversations, but could never make out the origin of the sounds or decipher what they were saying. He also "heard coughing and snoring and felt invisible entities brush past him as he entered a room."

There was a constant awareness "of being watched by unseen eyes." Only once did Sword report really observing a ghost. He was seated in the kitchen when, once again, he had a strange awareness "of being watched." He peered out the windows and beheld "the face of a young man wearing a floppy cap and a loose-fitting coat, looking back at him." Sword dashed to the window, but the form walked away and vanished. He believed he could identify this phantom.

In 1878, a great steamer was smashed up by Point Lookout during a gale. Thirty-one crewmen died. The remains of Joseph Haney drifted up on the Point Lookout beach, and he was interred near where his corpse had been discovered. The description of Haney, as read in the newspapers of the day, corresponded exactly with that of the young man Sword had observed at his window.

Another structure on the grounds situated directly across the road from the Confederate monument has also has been plagued by curious and spectral noises. This became such a common occurrence, parapsychologists from the Maryland Committee for Psychic Research, headed by noted parapsychologist Dr. Hans Holzer, in 1987 utilized Electronic Voice Phenomena or EVP to record the sounds.

Voices have been picked up on tape not audible while the recording session took place. It is widely believed in psychic circles that the utterances made out are those of the departed. EVP has been tried out in several locations in the United States. "One of the most interesting tests took place at a spot called Point Lookout," stated parapsychologists.

A collection of people involved in investigating hauntings undertook the EVP approach at Point Lookout. Tape recorders were placed at locations where the spectral noises had regularly been recounted. Although no voices were made out while the recording sessions took place, those investigating thought they could discern indistinct voices and other noises on their tapes when they were replayed.

One recording featured what, "sounded exactly like the whistle of a steamboat," a familiar sound around Point Lookout in past decades, though the use of steamboats had ceased many years before the EVP investigation. Men's taped voices appear to say such things as "living in the lighthouse," "going home," and "fire if they get too close." A woman's voice seemed to be saying, "vaccine" while another sounded like, "Let us not take objections to what they are doing."

Several other ghostly manifestations have been recounted in all sections of the lighthouse, in particular the cellar and an upstairs room. The smallest upstairs bedroom once had a revolting smell, only at night. Many inhabitants tried in vain to scour away the abhorrent stench characterized as "rotten."

Holzer's crew of psychics thought that this room had been employed to hold prisoners during the War, "women accused of spying or aiding the enemy in particular." Holzer maintained that the odor could have meant death or conflict or a person wrongfully held against their will until they died. Astonishingly, the decaying smell vanished after Holzer put forth his explanation.

Included in Point Lookout's ghostly denizens is a woman attired "in a long blue skirt and white blouse. Her misty form is most often seen standing at the top of the lighthouse stairs." Rangers think her to be Ann Davis, wife of the first keeper and keeper herself for thirty years after her husband's death. Ann's voice is believed to be the female voice taped by the research team on the tower stairway.

Ann tells visitors the lighthouse is "my home." Her lamentations are made out, particularly at night when the lighthouse would have been lit if it had not been deserted as a navigational aid. Rangers think Ann is mourning the active loss of the sentinel.

The most amazing occurrence took place when a woman employed by the State of Maryland resided in the deserted lighthouse.

She claimed to have felt comfortable with the spirits and thought she was appreciated by them. "One night after she had gone to bed, she was awakened by a ring of small lights whirling around in the ceiling over her," it was reported. A short time thereafter, she sniffed smoke, raced downstairs, and discovered a heater on fire.

She never beheld the spectral lights again but thought they materialized deliberately to guard her and to keep the lighthouse from burning.[44]

The beacon last shone in 1965, and the lighthouse has remained unoccupied since that time.

Or has it?

NORTH CAROLINA

BALD HEAD OLD BALDY" LIGHT

Located on Bald Head Island since 1817, the "Old Baldy" Light is North Carolina's oldest standing lighthouse. At one hundred and ten-feet tall, the light has lightning protection due to its height. Listed in the National Historic Register, it marks the entrance to Cape Fear River. Bald Head Island was originally proposed as a permanent site for the United Nations. Bald Head Island is only accessible by ferry.

Contact: Bald Head Island Information Center, P.O. Box 5069, Bald Head Island, North Carolina 28461. (910) 457-5000.

Bald Head "Old Baldy" Light,
Courtesy of Donna Ray Mitchell

Donna Ray Mitchell of the Old Baldy Foundation writes that this haunting is not only linked to the daughter of Aaron Burr, Theodosia Burr Alston, but also the Battle of Cloden from the Revolutionary War:

"The only haunting on Bald Head Island . . . is a little story about friends . . . staying in one of the keeper's cottages for the now demolished Cape Fear Light. . . . The mother had heard many a strange noise but attributed those to the constant wind. One day she heard the screen door open and close . . . [and] went to check . . . her son was busy playing on the floor. . . . She asked him: 'What was that?' "He replied, 'Oh, just Cloden . . . He comes to play sometimes."

"We repeated this story with a chill . . . but the real thrill came when we learned through research that the Scottish battle over Bonny Prince Charles (whose wife Flora, reportedly waited for his arrival . . . on Bald Head Island) was fought on the Battlefield of Cloden."[45]

In another letter, Ms. Ray Mitchell writes of an encounter experienced by her former teacher:

"My high school trigonometry teacher, a person of whom I would never doubt, and her husband were riding in a golf cart (Bald Head Island's primary form of transportation) toward the east on the Main Island Road that skirts the dunes."

It was late. They both detected an odd odor. "It wasn't quite perfume but more like incense," she wrote. The former teacher and her husband saw what looked to be "a woman walking in their direction in the median." Because of the dark, they could not make out her face, but "she seemed to be wearing a hooded cape that floated around her." They were paralyzed in their cart "and became spooked." When they turned around and looked for her again, there was no hint of the mysterious woman.

An artist, Rusty Hughes, who lives in Southport, swears he has seen the ghost of a woman wearing white twice, both times while walking on the beach at night.[46]

Further reference to the haunted woman is this account from *The Charlotte News*, where both Nags Head and Bald Head Island lay claim to the ghost of Theodosia Burr Alston:

> "Nags Head . . . and Bald Head, the strange island in the lower Cape Fear, ghoulishly claim to be the habitat of the ghost of beautiful Theodosia Burr Alston, daughter of Aaron Burr and wife of an early governor of South Carolina."

Theodosia, set on seeing her father in Baltimore just after his treason trial against the United States, obtained passage on *The Patriot* out of Charleston. Two days at sea, the sloop encountered an immense storm. Both *The Patriot*, the crew, and all passengers, including Theodosia Burr Alston, were never heard from again.

Many years ago, the portrait of a "handsome woman" was discovered in a fisherman's shack on Nags Head. The "handsome woman" was recognized to be the long lost Theodosia. Locals held Nags Head to be the final resting place of *The Patriot* and "her lovely cargo," according to *The Charlotte News* article.

Meanwhile at Bald Head, people were not buying Nags Head's claim to Theodosia, due to the fact that they felt the specter of Theodosia was securely incarcerated "among the dunes of the island, near where her ship went aground in the storm."

Storyteller and newspaperman Bill Keziah of Southport related this version of the story: "Aground on the Shoals off Bald Head, the sloop was boarded by pirates from the island, looted, and Theodosia was brought ashore, the prize of the pirate chief. He assigned three of his men to guard her . . . to prevent her escaping from the camp."

But Theodosia was said to have, indeed, escaped. The "three luckless guards" immediately were beheaded for allowing her to get away. She was soon recaptured and transported back to camp, but could not endure the confinement placed upon her. She died and was interred on Bald Head Island. It was then her specter was said to begin roaming the island, perpetually attempting escape.

The headless ghosts of the pirates also wander at night, forever searching for not only their lost heads but also Theodosia. These specters were fearless in their search. Years ago, a Coast Guardsman policing the beach at midnight "had the wits scared out of him by the three headless ghosts."

Keziah further contends that no man can walk across Bald Head at midnight with a "marvelously beautiful woman" without the headless ghosts of the three Spanish pirates approaching to look into her face to find if she is Theodosia Burr Alston.

In addition to Nags and Bald Head Islands and Cape Hatteras, Theodosia is said to make appearances at One If By Land Restaurant in New York City.

There is presently a bed and breakfast located on Bald Head island called Theodosia's, named for Aaron Burr's ill fated daughter.[47]

CAPE HATTERAS LIGHT

Located north of Cape Hatteras Point and erected in 1870, the Cape Hatteras Light, at one hundred and ninety-three feet, is the tallest lighthouse in the United States. It is in the National Historic Register and is an active aid to navigation in a National Park.

Contact: Cape Hatteras National Seashore, P.O. Box 190, Buxton, North Carolina 27920. (919) 995-4474.

Cape Hatteras Light was on *Lighthouse Digest's* Doomsday List of endangered lighthouses, but has been moved back from its current site and the encroaching sea just in time for the 1999 hurricane season.

The light was discontinued in 1936 due to the encroachment of the sea, replaced by an automatic light on a steel skeleton tower one hundred and sixty-six feet above sea level on a sand dune. The shoreline in front of the old lighthouse had eroded from 2,000 feet to less than 150 feet. The organization Move the Lighthouse maintained that the only way to save the historic structure was to move it back, much the same way as Block Island (Southeast) Light was moved. Cape Hatteras Light was indeed moved back in 1999.[48]

Cape Hatteras Light, *Courtesy of Walter H. Cushman*

Both Bald Head and Cape Hatteras Lighthouses lay claim to the ghost of Theodosia Burr Alston, who "wanders across dunes, sighing woefully with the wind, looking for escape or rising from the surf in a shimmering emerald-green dress."[49]

GEORGIA

ST. SIMONS LIGHTHOUSE

Located on St. Simons Island, the original lighthouse was built in 1811 of tabby blocks, a North African and Iberian composition of oyster shells, water, and lime (otherwise referred to as coquina). It is one hundred and six feet high and utilized a Third Order Fresnel lens that could be seen eighteen miles at sea.

Contact: Museum of Coastal History, P.O. Box 21136, St. Simons Island, Georgia 31522. (912) 638-4666.

St. Simons Island Light, *Courtesy of Walter H. Cushman*

The tower and outbuildings were wrecked by the Confederates in 1862. When the reconstruction commenced many years later, a strange malady struck many of the work crew. Even the contractor grew ill and perished. As a result, all labor stopped.

A bondsmen, wishing to safeguard his stake, resumed the work, but after a short illness, he too died. Reconstruction was not finished until the summer of 1872 and the lighthouse was finally back in service on the first of September of that year.

Many years later, Keeper Fred Osborne thought it necessary to hire an assistant keeper. Osborne, however, was known for being demanding. Few applicants applied for the position before he interviewed, and subsequently hired, John Stevens. Prior to applying for the job of assistant keeper, John Stevens had discovered the hapless record of the lighthouse.

In the beginning, the relationship between the men was compatible, to a point. As Osborne educated Stevens in many of the lesser responsibilities that were the assistant keeper's, however, it was quite clear that Osborne attended to the tower's Fresnel light with maniacal pride.

Discord grew between the two men and Stevens felt indignant about his superior. Reports made their way to the islanders that there were difficulties at the lighthouse.

In March, 1880, Fred Osborne came to relieve Stevens. A storm was coming in. Osborne examined a minute smear on one of the windows and accused Stevens of slipshod work. By this time, Stevens was on his last nerves. It was time to rectify their disputes.

Osborne pulled a pistol. Stevens ran back into the house and grabbed his shotgun and, as Osborne stepped forward, Stevens fired. Stevens transported Osborne to the Brunswick hospital, claiming the event to be accidental and returned to the lighthouse.

After many days of excruciating pain, Osborne died and the sheriff took Stevens into custody. But a gale that had been approaching finally came to pass. A decision had to made quickly. Hold John Stevens, thus leaving the lighthouse without a keeper, or let him temporarily assume his duties and chance his fleeing.

There was no other available keeper. After much discussion, it was thought that the protection of ships at sea was most important. They returned Stevens to the lighthouse to serve as keeper until his trial.

After the gale abated, the sheriff discovered the diligent Stevens still at the lighthouse. At the trial, Stevens maintained self-defense and, because there were no witnesses to say otherwise, he was vindicated.

Or was he?

John Stevens was now a different man. He often spoke of eerie noises. Those who came to visit, rather than frighten the jittery keeper, soon learned it prudent, before climbing to the top of the tower, to make their presence known by hailing him. During especially wild gales, he often heard the weighty thump of footfalls. They would make it to the second platform, the third, the fourth, and finally the fifth and last.

Until his death, John Stevens thought he heard the ghostly footfalls of dead keeper Osborne lugging himself painfully up the spiral stairs.

Although the lighthouse is no longer in use, visitors still describe the sound of heavy footfalls in the old tower, and many swear they get a whiff of the kerosene used in the old-fashioned lamp as they climb the cast iron stairs.[50]

The heavy footsteps heard on the spiral stairway leading up to the beacon chamber are so loud, they can sometimes be heard from neighboring cottages.

In 1907, Carl Svendsen, his wife, and their dog, Jinx, took the position of lightkeepers on the island. Mrs. Svendsen, as a matter of course, put dinner on the table when she heard her husband rattling down the tower steps from the light room. One night when she thought she heard him and put his dinner down, the footsteps reached the ground, but her husband did not appear. Jinx barked and moaned in fear. Mrs. Svendsen explored and discovered her husband was still at the top of the tower.

Svendsen did not believe his wife's story, at first. Soon thereafter, "he also heard the phantom footsteps," according to *The Lighthouse*. As the years went by, they often heard the "ghost" with no clue as to its identity. The Svendsens tended the light for forty years, and, in that time, came to accept the curiosity. Jinx, however, continued to be horrified and "would hide whenever the strange footsteps clattered and echoed around tower." To this day, footsteps can still be heard on the steps, especially when the weather is stormy.[51]

Perhaps it is Keeper Osborne, still held to his duties, ensuring that the light is always lit.

SOUTH CAROLINA

GEORGETOWN (NORTH ISLAND) LIGHT

Located on North Island at the Winyah Bay Entrance, Georgetown (North Island) Light was erected in 1867. It is listed in the National Historic Register and is an active aid to navigation.

Contact: Captain Sandy's Tours, Inc., P.O. Box 2533, Pawleys Island, South Carolina 29585. (803) 527-4106.

Georgetown Light, *Courtesy of Walter H. Cushman*

Because of the history of wild storms slamming against tiny North Island, in the early 1800s a massive stone lighthouse was built there. According to the article "Discover Why Georgetown is Called the Ghost Capital of the United States," a keeper resided there with his "small, fair-haired daughter, Annie." For provisions, they rowed across the bay into the bustling port of Georgetown.

One afternoon, after a trip to town, they filled their tiny craft and set off for home. Forbidding clouds collected overhead and heaped rain and hail on their small craft. The wind became more powerful and produced fierce waves. A quarter of the trip still to be made, their boat flooded.

In desperation, the keeper tied his cherished daughter to his back and attempted to swim for it. In shock and exhausted, he did not remember making shore. Many hours later, the keeper woke to discover his drowned daughter still fastened to his back.

The keeper was never the same after the death of his little girl. For some time after, he roamed the Georgetown streets, "sad and disoriented, calling out the name of his dead child."

From that time on, sailors have told tales of a "sweet blonde child" who appeared on their boat as they headed out into the bay. Though this usually happened on calm, sunny days, she urged them to "go back." These entreaties always preceded wild, unanticipated storms. It has been said that "those who ignore her well-timed warnings soon find themselves facing a watery grave."[52]

Decades ago, a young boy, now an accomplished captain commanding a great commercial boat, was at work on a shrimp trawler in the Atlantic off North Island. Briefly alone at his job, and determined to do it briskly, the boy instantly snapped his head up when a motion caught his eye.

Positioned by the boat's deck was a young girl. His description: "Her long, blond hair was caught up with a pink ribbon. The ruffled hem of her pink ankle-length dress moved gently with the faint ocean breeze. In her hand, the girl held a cloth doll."

He was too astonished to speak. The girl stared hard at him and said: "Go back." She lifted her arm and pointed toward the jetties, again demanding, "Go back."

The boy dropped his work and bolted to tell the captain, who was making ready to turn the trawler east, out to sea. "Thank you, son," the captain said softly. "We'll be heading in now."

To all ships that sailed by within hailing range, the captain shouted: "Bad storm coming! Head on in." But his caution went unheeded. No other ship captains wished to desert such good shrimping on a calm day due to predictions of inclement weather.

Late in the day, dark clouds assembled quickly. A stiff breeze blew. The rising tide almost hid the massive granite, jetty rocks, with only the jagged stone points noticeable above the swirling water. Beautiful North Island darkened together with the rapidly blackening sky. The base of the lighthouse was ghostly pale against the dark trees, its beacon shining brightly. The boy leaned against the rail and looked seriously at the lighthouse.

Perplexed and deep in thought, he did not notice the captain's steps behind him. The older gentleman nodded his gray head toward the lighthouse.

"That was her home," he said. The captain heard the story of the keeper's daughter when he was a young man. He knew the spirit of the girl cautioned sailors when a fierce storm was fixing to sweep into the bay. That is why he took the boy's incredible story so seriously.

By nightfall, the gale had attained a dreadful crescendo. Many lives and boats were lost. The boy never got over "his chilling experience" or the captain's story. Now a gray-bearded captain with his own flourishing commercial boat, he can oftentimes be coaxed to tell of the day he met the specter of the little girl from the North Island Lighthouse.[53]

HAIG POINT (RANGE REAR) LIGHT

Located on Daufuskie Island and Caliboque Sound, ten miles from Savannah, Georgia, Haig Point (Range Rear) Light was erected in 1872 and relit in 1986. The light is a private aid to navigation and is listed in the National Historic Register. Daufuskie, an Native American name, is one of the oldest islands on the eastern seaboard.

Contact: Haig Point: (800) 992-3635 or (803) 686-4244.

A private residence, Haig Point (Range Rear) Light is located on an island filled with mystery and adventure. There are no unauthorized cars allowed on Daufuskie Island.

Some of the earliest known ceramics, dating back to 2,000 B.C. have been found on the island. Bloody Point, at the island's southern tip, was the site of the Yamasee Indian War in 1759, a battle in which the British wiped out the last few Native Americans along the coast. The wildlife of the island includes deer, alligator, and ibis.

During World War II, a Nazi submarine was spotted off Daufuskie Island by a beach patrol.

Rich in black history and home to the unique Gullah culture, the island may soon become just another resort. Developers are creating luxury residences and golf courses. The indigenous black population is being displaced.

From roughly 1865, when General Sherman gave the island to newly freed slaves, until 1985, the island population remained almost completely black and was virtually cut off from the rest of the world. As a result, inhabitants developed a Gullah dialect and culture heavily influenced by African languages and customs.

By 1959, pollution in the Savannah River put an end to the island's oyster business. The young people left and did not return. In the mid 1970s, Daufuskie's population was estimated at only forty inhabitants. By 1990, its permanent population was up to eighty, mostly due to the influx of white business people and a few blacks who returned from the north.

The two largest developers, the Melrose Company and International Paper, say they have not displaced anyone, because the plantation they developed has long been uninhabited. But the private roads and plantation gates are an abomination to residents accustomed to roaming the island.

The Mary Field Elementary School, made famous by Pat Conroy in his autobiographical novel, *The Water is Wide*, is the only school on the island. Houses with gabled hatches were brought from the Caribbean by British planters and remain the dominant island style. Some shutters are painted "haint blue," a bright, lurid shade that locals believe wards off haints (disembodied living beings who disturb your sleep).

The Haig Point (Range Rear) Lighthouse has withstood gales, tornadoes, hurricanes, and earthquakes. In 1879, white picket fences were installed around the lights to prevent damage to the facilities and bluff by roaming Daufuskie cattle.[54]

The light held special interest to twelve-year-old Nick Beatty, whose family lived in the lighthouse. The boy was fascinated with Daufuskie since the time he and his family moved there. With the exception of intermittent outings with his family and days in the Daufuskie two-room school, Nick's existence was much the same as a child who might have lived on a South Carolina coastal island a hundred years ago.

Nick, his sister, and brother enjoyed exploring the beach. What they especially liked was the spooky old cemetery where stained headstones, a few wildly lopsided, indicated the oldest graves.

Nick's parents often made trips to the mainland. When he stayed behind, Sal, a friend of the family, looked after Nick and his two siblings. Once when Nick and Sal were alone, footfalls were heard in the hall overhead, nearing the stairs. Slowly, as if someone might be clutching the rail, the footfalls could be heard starting down the steps.

The footfalls paused, and neither Sal nor Nick budged. For a moment, all was quiet. Then they began again. This time, though, it seemed as if they were starting at the upper landing. Nick gripped Sal's hand hard. He was aware of how many steps there were and began to count. Four more to go, three, two, and now the last step. It was in the room with them. Nick and Sal looked over at the foot of the steps, but no one was there.

A chair in the room suddenly started to slowly rock back and forth. Sal rose as if he would seize it, but the instant he started toward it, the rocking stopped.

Weeks later, Nick told his mother stories of old shipwrecks that had happened near the island, and of a terrible Indian massacre at the north end of Daufuskie. His mother demanded to know the source of these wild tales. He said Arthur, an elderly man with white hair and beard, who often visited him. Nick was perplexed when his mother responded that no, she had never seen Arthur.

One day, when his mother was asking one of the islanders about the history of the house, she began to guess who Nick's "friend" really was. Just to be sure, she decided to go by the cemetery on her way home. On a simple, gray granite marker was engraved the name Arthur Burns. Burns had been keeper of the light for many years.

Sometime after his retirement, Arthur Burns had become quite ill and was taken from the island to a hospital on the mainland. When he returned, he vowed no one would ever get him to leave his house again.

All that really mattered to Nick was that he had a friend named Arthur who could tell the most fascinating stories a boy had ever heard. The ghost of the old man with the white beard enjoyed a special friendship with Nick. The rest of the Beatty family saw him too, in the kitchen, and on another occasion walking through the yard.

Did the spirit of Arthur find a sympathetic soul in young Nick out there in the old cemetery and decide to go home with him? There are those who believe that the spirits of the deceased may sometimes be present in the cemetery where they have been buried.

HILTON HEAD RANGE REAR (LEAMINGTON) LIGHT

Located on Hilton Head Island, the ninety-five-foot tall, skeleton cast-iron tower was constructed in 1880. Listed in the National Historic Register, the Hilton Head Range Rear (Leamington) Light stands on the grounds of the Palmetto Dunes residential community and resort.

Contact: Greenwood Development Corporation, P.O. Box 5268, Hilton Head Island, South Carolina 29938. (803) 785-1106.

Hilton Head Range Rear Light, *Courtesy of Carolyn Ortiz*

Hilton Head Range Rear (Leamington) Light has withstood the forces of nature over the years, including a severe earthquake in 1887 and numerous hurricanes.

The spectral "Lady in the Blue Dress" or "Blue Lady of Hilton Head" is well known in the Outer Banks, dating to the hurricane of August 1898.

According to *South Carolina Ghosts*, for three days hurricane warnings were announced. At Hilton Head Island, the job of keeping the light lit through the gale fell to Adam Fripp, keeper for three years, widower for two. He was assisted by his twenty-one-year-old daughter, Caroline. The hurricane headed directly for the South Atlantic coast.

When the hurricane hit, Caroline fought through the fierce wind and rain to bring her father his dinner in the tower. She loaded up with food, knowing Fripp would need it during the long night. The hurricane worsened. Caroline took a look at the barometer. She had never seen such a low reading. Even their dog, Frisky, seemed to detect the advancing gale.

Up in the tower, the hurricane blew out one of the windows. Fripp got several boards to cover the exposed windows against the building storm, but they didn't stay in place. Another window exploded. Torrents of rain came roaring through the open windows. At two minutes before six, the light went out.

In the darkness, Caroline made her way into the storage room and found a torch. For two hours, Fripp tried to light the lamp, but each time the wind blew it out. He and Caroline were soaked through with sea water.

At one point, Caroline called to her father to try to light the lamp again, but there was no reply.

She discovered the torch on the floor and lit it. As the gleam of the lamp illuminated the small room, Caroline beheld her father lying almost at her feet, clenching his chest in agony, unable to speak.

Caroline dragged him toward the door to the lighthouse stairs, but her father was unable to even inch down the stairs. Caroline thought it better to wait for the morning, and so they tried to sleep.

When she awoke, Caroline could not hear the wind nor the rain. She thought it best to venture outside to assess the destruction of the hurricane. Inside the tower it was pitch black, so Caroline made her way down by counting the steps. As she reached the last step, her foot plunged into water. The sea water was about two feet deep within the tower. This meant that the island was flooded about four feet, perhaps even more.

The cattle and pigs, her dog Frisky, and the other people, what happened to them? When could she get her father home now that the storm was past? It would be risky for him to attempt to walk to the house through water this high. Caroline knew she must summon a doctor. The wind picked up outside while the rain blasted against the metal lighthouse. The hurricane returned, full force.

In less than an hour, the sea had risen almost another foot. Caroline quickly returned to her father, still asleep. She fell into an exhausted sleep and when she awoke, it was daylight. The storm had passed. Caroline gazed out one of the broken windows.

The island was under water, but miraculously their house still stood. They had to return home fast but also had to clean the light for the night. Caroline worked quickly, replacing the wet wick. She noticed that her father's fingers shook. How could he handle the steps? Fripp held onto the rail as he went down, and Caroline hovered close by. Once at the bottom of the tower, Fripp grappled to open the door.

She heard her father's cry. Adam Fripp was having a heart attack. Caroline waded through the water, encouraging him along. She knew that if he fell into the water, she would be unable to lift him out. Her father clutched the skirt of her dress in his hand to prevent himself from slipping below the water's surface. Caroline felt the edge of the porch hard against her back. Turning, she was able to push the upper part of her father's body over it. After he rested, Fripp was able to pull himself up with Caroline's help. The exertion so fatigued him that he wished to rest. She placed a blanket over him.

Island fisherman Donald Stuart emerged in a small dinghy and Caroline cried out to him. Together they hoisted her father into his bed.

"Mr. Stuart, could you get a doctor?" Caroline implored.

Stuart replied: "I've got to keep lookin' for my two older children . . . My wife and baby drowned last night." And he continued his sad search.

Caroline had a troubled sleep, permeated with nightmares of the house being swept out to sea, fighting to save her father, while all around them in the water people were pleading for aid. In the late afternoon, she awoke to the rays of the sun warm upon her face through the window.

After she lit the lamp, Caroline noticed something yellow in the water by the steps of the lighthouse. It was a doll still gripped by a dead child.

When she returned to her father's bedroom, he was still in the same position as when she had left him. Caroline called him, but he did not respond. Adam Fripp was dead. Caroline stated to cry wildly.

The next morning, Stuart was at the door. Noticing that the light was out and learning that Adam Fripp had died, he came with two other islanders bearing a sea chest to serve as a coffin. They weighted the chest, took it into the ocean, and left it beyond the low-water mark. "Die by water, lie by water," Stuart said as they lowered the chest over the side.

One of the womenfolk attempted to get Caroline to come home with her, but she refused to leave the house. Oftentimes at night, Caroline was seen walking between her home and the lighthouse, calling her father. She always wore the same long, blue dress that she had worn on the night of the hurricane. But the dress had grown torn and bedraggled. It was obvious she would not outlast the shock and anguish of the storm. A few weeks later, Caroline died.

Since then, on wild and stormy nights, a girl is seen in one of the lighthouse windows or at the foot of it. A young policewoman who patrols that part of the island said that the "Blue Lady is reported most often during hurricane season. . . . people . . . swear they've seen her. Others . . . heard the sound of a woman sobbing not far from where the keeper's house once stood. . . . I wouldn't go near that old lighthouse on windy, rainy nights."

The lady in the blue dress walks still, searching for her dead father in the storms that followed her death.[55]

FLORIDA

BOCA GRANDE LIGHT

Located at Gasparilla Island in the Gulf of Mexico, Boca Grande Light was erected in 1890. It is listed in the National Historic Register, is an active aid to navigation, and is located in a state park.

Contact: Gasparilla Island State Recreation Area, Gulf Boulevard, Boca Grande, Florida 33921. (941) 964-0375.

Boca Grande Light, *Courtesy of Walter H. Cushman*

Much like the headless pirates on Bald Head Island, Gasparilla Island not only features pirates, but also a beloved and beheaded princess.

Locals think the remains of a lovely Spanish princess are interred by the old lighthouse and that her "headless apparition occasionally appears on the beach," in search of her lost head, according to *Guide to Florida Lighthouses*.

The island of Gasparilla was named after an infamous, violent, womanizing, money hungry pirate.[56] Jose Gaspar is said to have utilized the island as a retreat. He was a man of extreme avarice and brutality, inclined to angry outbursts. He interred his many female victims on a tiny island a few miles south of Boca Grande.

During one of Gaspar's trips, he seized a ship with a ravishing Spanish princess aboard, Josefa. As he navigated to Gasparilla Island with his beautiful prize, he implored her to take his hand in marriage. Josefa not only turned him down, but also cursed the pirate and spat in his face. Her humiliation of him was the final blow. In a fit of rage, he beheaded her.

Gaspar lamented his impetuous deed and gently transported the princess ashore at Gasparilla Island where he entombed her in the sand. However, he kept Josefa's head, enshrined in a jar. Afterwards, many have claimed that a headless figure wanders the beach at Gasparilla Island searching for its missing head.

Port Boca Grande Lighthouse was deserted in 1967. Locals, intent on saving the beacon, had it transferred from federal to county ownership on February 11, 1972, for inclusion in a park. The Conservation and Improvement Association shouldered the costs of repairing the fast-decaying edifice. With the help of the Coast Guard, the original imported Fresnel lens was reinstalled. On November 21, the beacon was relit.[57]

A letter from Joyce Healy-Volpe relates that Boca Grande translates to "big mouth."

"While Jose Gaspar is a very big deal over on the Gulf side of Florida," Healy-Volpe writes, "every year there's a big Gasparilla Festival in the Tampa Bay area. It is said that one of his female victims, now a headless body, roams the beach near the Port Boca Grande Light."[58]

PENSACOLA LIGHTHOUSE

Located at the entrance of Pensacola Bay on an island six miles southeast of Miami, Pensacola Lighthouse was constructed in 1859. One hundred and seventy-one feet high, Pensacola Lighthouse is listed in the National Historic Register and is an active aid to navigation on a naval air station.

Contact: Pensacola Historical Society, 405 Adams Street, Pensacola, Florida 32501. (850) 434-5455.

Blood stains and pipe smoke play an important part in this alleged haunting.

Sandra Johnson, Curator/Director of the Pensacola Historical Society, writes that "there is a ghost at the lighthouse. He is known for throwing things at people who stay in the lighthouse keepers' quarters. He also laughs at people, slams doors and moves things."

Items that are left downstairs in the keeper's quarters mysteriously materialize upstairs.

The specter is thought to be the first lighthouse keeper, Jeremiah Ingraham. Ingraham passed away mysteriously in the lighthouse tower and his wife became keeper. His ghost makes himself known, according to many eyewitnesses. Stains on the floor in the keeper's quarters are thought to be blood. Many think it might be Ingraham's blood.[59]

Elaborating on Johnson's letter, one hundred years ago the first keeper, Jeremiah Ingraham, was stabbed to death by his wife in the lighthouse tower. Her penance for the dastardly crime was to ascend the lighthouse stairs, shouldering her husband's responsibility until the end of her days.

In the midst of the recent refurbishing of the keeper's quarters, workmen unearthed "blood-like stains" in the southwest bedroom of the quarters. The pine wood floor had been hidden for years beneath felt and vinyl tiles.

"The stains are definitely blood," stated construction supervisor Leo Glenn. "One dark splotch, about a foot in length, lies to the left of the fireplace, while quarter-sized splatters lie to the right, with more splatters lying across the room.

"We figured there was a bed here in the middle, and they fought all the way around the bed," he noted. "Blood darkens it like cherry wood. It just soaks through. Now, a normal juice stain, you can wash out."

Regardless of whether a murder did indeed take place, Cultural Resource Manager Dick Callaway of the Naval Air Station, which leases the light from the Coast Guard said, "There are many other unexplained phenomena."

During restoration of the keeper's quarters, odd events took place. One workman was holding a water hose that was wrenched out of his hand, others detected the odor of pipe tobacco. None of the workmen smoked a pipe.

There have been cold chills felt on hot days, a spectral form has been spotted in the window of the lighthouse when the structure was tightly locked up, and a back door to the keeper's quarters has been repeatedly opened, in spite of it being locked.

Objects are hurled by the phantom at those who stay in the keeper's quarters. Spectral laughing is heard as well as the sound of slamming doors. Many of these events have been witnessed by at least two or more people.

The Navy elected to safeguard the stains with a transparent sealer and polyurethane paint that would enable visitors to the newly re-furbished keeper's quarters to study the stains and come to their own conclusions as to their origin.

Area officials have proposed that the stains be analyzed to learn if they are blood. In order to do so, some of the floorboards would have to be torn up and shipped to outside labs for DNA testing. Emmett Hatten, who was raised at the lighthouse in the 1930s when his father was keeper, stated that his mother scoured that stain to remove it but never could. His mother consistently referred to it as blood.[60]

ST. AUGUSTINE LIGHT

Located on Anastasia Island and constructed in 1874, St. August-ine Light was the first official lighthouse in Florida, in America's oldest city (founded in 1565). The one hundred and sixty-one foot tower's lighting mechanism was destroyed by Confederate soldiers during the Civil War. The light, a Fourth Order Fresnel lens, is listed in the National Historic Register and is an active aid to navigation.

Contact: St. Augustine Lighthouse Museum, 81 Lighthouse Avenue, St. Augustine, Florida 32084. (904) 829-0745.

St. Augustine Light, *Courtesy of Walter H. Cushman*

Cold spots have been felt and objects move from one place to another, especially in the location of the gift shop at the St. Augustine Light. A ghostly figure in a fancy dress was witnessed by at least two persons around 1965.

A man named Dan was renting the keeper's quarters. During the night, he was awakened and chilled by the sight of a young girl in a long, lacy dress standing in the doorway. After several moments, she faded away.

A friend who visited Dan and was quartered in the same bedroom. The next morning, he told how he was spooked by the same spectral figure. Dan suspected they had seen the apparition of one of the keeper's daughters who had drowned somewhere near the lighthouse.

Sometime after the light was automated, David Swain, a light tender, found the light mysteriously off in the middle of the night. When he investigated, he found nothing wrong except that the switch was turned off. He simply turned it back on. This happened three nights in a row.

Swain speculated that Andreau, a keeper in the 1850s, was responsible for turning the light off, and following him up the steps. Andreau is believed to have fallen to his death while painting the original light tower.[61]

Swain said that every time he walked from the keeper's house to the tower, footsteps would follow him. The footsteps followed him up the tower and back. Swain said he could "hear the rocks a-crunchin," but no one ever came into the house.

Another man said he and his wife saw lights coming from the shell of the keeper's house, which burned down in 1970.

St. Augustine Light Burned-out Keeper's Quarters, *Courtesy of the St. Augustine Lighthouse*

St. Augustine Light Renovations, *Courtesy of the St. Augustine Lighthouse*

A malevolent force appeared to be at work, or in opposition to work-men, at the St. Augustine Light. John A. Lienlockker took part in the beginning reconstruction of the incinerated lightkeeper's quarters. He recounted numerous peculiar events that took place in the old brick building. While attempting to rip out a tree stump, a chain snapped, whipping through the back window of a truck and barely missing his partner's head.

"These and additional phenomenon during the six-month restora-tion disturbed John and his partners, Wayne Pierce and Michael Gourley, enough to create dread about working there," Lienlockker recounted.

"The most frightening occurrence happened while all three were precariously balanced on the rickety porch when, out of nowhere, a big spike came shooting down from a beam and hit the big guy. It almost knocked us all off," Lienlockker said.

The "big guy" was Wayne, who withstood the blow better than Lienlockker or Gourley could have. They bandaged Wayne and took him to the hospital. John said they all had the feeling that "something didn't want them working there."[62]

LOUISIANA

SABINE PASS LIGHT

It is located at the northeast Texas border on the Louisiana side where the Sabine and Neches rivers join as they flow to the Gulf of Mexico Pass. Built in 1856, it is in the National Historic Register and on *Lighthouse Digest's* Endangered List.

In 1886, a hurricane sent a surge of water twenty miles inland, killing one hundred and fifty residents of Sabine Pass and practically destroying the town. Everything near the lighthouse was destroyed except the tower with its eighteen-inch thick walls and its eight buttresses.

The lighthouse had been sending its beam of light for less than ten years when the Civil War broke out. Late in 1862, a squadron of Union troops successfully entered Sabine Lake and destroyed Fort Sabine. A month later they were routed by the Confederates. The Union troops fled, losing two ships and one hundred men. The lens was hit by a cannonball, which broke part of it.

The keeper repaired the broken lens by gluing the front and back covers of the Bible together and placing them between the two broken parts of the lens. The repaired lens was then removed from the lighthouse by Keeper Granger, who hid it in the town of Sabine Pass until the war was over.

Sam Monroe, president of the Port Arthur Historical Society, believes the specter that dwells in the house is a soldier slain in the well-known Battle of Sabine Pass.

In the early 1950s, a caretaker requested a discharge from his position. He had beheld the ghost of a man attired in a bold, brass-buttoned black suit and cap that appeared to be the attire of a prior lighthouse keeper.[63]

The apparition repeatedly dropped in on the caretaker at that time, appearing at his bedside wearing a dark-colored suit with the lighthouse insignia on the jacket and the emblem of the old U.S. Lighthouse Service on his hat. After numerous appearances by the ghost, caretakers were never assigned back to the lighthouse, presumably because of the sightings.[64]

In 1952, the Coast Guard notified Keeper Steven Purgley that the light would be extinguished and torn down. Furious, Purgley started the Sabine Pass Lighthouse Association to save the lighthouse. Eventually, it became the property of the Louisiana Wildlife and Fisheries Commission. In 1986, the General Service Administration auctioned the light for $55,000. It was bought by two businessmen who thought it might be an ideal restaurant or yacht club.

But nothing was ever done to preserve or restore this historic beacon. The light is deserted, although many times major plans have called for the renovation of the area as a recreational site.[65]

CHAPTER IV

PACIFIC COAST LIGHTHOUSES

CALIFORNIA

BATTERY POINT (CRESCENT CITY) LIGHT

Located at Battery Point Island, Battery Point (Crescent City) Light was erected in 1856 and reactivated in 1982. A private aid to navigation, the light is listed in the National Historic Register.

Contact: Nancy Schneider, P.O. Box 535, Crescent City, California 95531. (707) 464-3089.

Battery Point (Crescent City) Light, *Courtesy of Walter H. Cushman*

Our first Pacific Coast lighthouse; Battery Point (Crescent City) is accessible only at low tide. A great tidal wave, or tsunami, swept away most of the town of Crescent City in 1964.

Lighthouse pen pal Hazel Voleck sent me a pamphlet about Battery Point that she picked up many years ago when she visited the light. The pamphlet was written by Nadine Tugel who, with her husband, Jerry, was a keeper at Battery Point Light for about nine years. They are now retired. In the pamphlet, Nadine related that a college group inspected the lighthouse in the 1960s with equipment that detects ghosts. They described three entities: two adults and a child. Many believe that one is Captain DeWolf of the ill-fated ship, the *Brother Jonathan*; the other, Captain John Jeffrey, was keeper for over thirty-eight years. No one knows who the child is and there is no record of anyone dying at the site.

Subsequent to the probe, curious events began taking place, affecting the Tugels. Furniture moved. Objects broke without reason. Many of the occurrences took place during turbulent, foggy weather. Footsteps have also been heard over the years, heading to the tower resolutely on the hour, "as if someone was going to check the beacon," according to the pamphlet, *Battery Point Lighthouse: Ghosts, Dragons, Mermaids.*

During one gale, the keeper and his wife were roused from their beds by footsteps, but the burglar alarm over the door in the keeper's room had not rung. The keeper, feeling spooked, investigated the service room, hoisted the hatch door, and discovered the light was out. He replaced the bulb and the rest of the night was peaceful. In the morning, the alarm was inspected. It was working just fine. Why had the alarm not sounded?

A rocking chair that used to be in the living room was, at that time, in the captain's memorial room. Former keepers complained that the chair would rock when no one was in it and the room would smell of pipe smoke. One gentleman came out to the lighthouse saying:

"I'll visit you during the day, but don't expect me to come out at night."

The gentleman and a friend had previously remained at the lighthouse to relieve the keepers. After retiring to bed, they were roused by organ music. Twice they heard it, but after a search, the playing ceased. They left abruptly, never to return at night.

One couple with two children lived there for a year. The man did not care for island life or the light, but the rest of his family loved it. He wanted to leave, she wanted to stay. One morning, he woke up and heard the words:

"Get the hell off the island and stay off." His son, sleeping downstairs, also heard the same directive. The family moved to the mainland and the couple separated. While the mother and her now-grown children still visit the lighthouse, the father will not.

The Tugels heard numerous tales from them about items that moved, lost articles that reappeared in unexpected locations, broken objects, and phones that rang in the night, all without explanation.

One day, when Nadine was working in the radiator room, a crash sounded in the living room. She discovered the cranberry glass chimney from an antique candle holder broken on the floor in the empty room.

Another time, Tugel noticed a woman in a tour group standing in the doorway to the tower stepping to one side and looking up the stairway. At the end of the tour, the woman called Nadine aside and said: "I believe you have ghosts." The woman related how, as she was standing there, she had a feeling that someone placed a hand on her side as if wishing to go by her. When the woman turned around, there was no one there. A year later, another person on a tour had an almost identical experience while standing in the same area.

Nadine once woke at midnight, making out a man and woman talking, but could not decipher their conversation. She woke her husband, telling him she heard voices. They rose and investigated the lighthouse and the island, but not detecting anymore conversations or locating anyone who could have made them, they returned to bed. Around three in the morning, Jerry woke up, hearing the same muffled voices Nadine heard at midnight. "The woman would giggle at something the man had said . . . the voices were from the captain's room . . . all coincided with what I had heard only the location was different," Nadine related.

Once when Nadine and Jerry visited the mainland, they made sure to lock the lighthouse and set the burglar alarm before they left. They returned at night and went right to bed.

Jerry remarked how cold the bed was. There was a spot about an inch and a half in diameter by Nadine's foot that "was as warm as toast." Jerry wondered why "they" did not warm up his side. The next night the same thing occurred, obligingly, on his side of the bed.

Another night they were almost asleep when they felt a whack on their bed. Nadine thought the cat had jumped up, but it was locked in the radio room. Jerry wished "they" would leave him and Nadine to the privacy of their room.

Every night, Jerry would put his slippers beside the bed, ready to jump into them if an emergency arose. One night, they discovered the slippers turned in the opposite direction. He thought Nadine was teasing him and told her to stop moving his slippers around. But Nadine knew nothing about it.

One winter, friends visited them for a few days. Nadine mentioned the ghost stories but her friend balked at talk of ghosts. In the morning, Nadine was preparing breakfast, and her friend had gone upstairs to dress. When she returned, her friend asked who wanted to use the bathroom. No one had been up there. The friend had heard footsteps come up to the bathroom door. When they stopped, she said: "You can't come in." There was no reply.

Many times during their visit, the friend would ask if anyone had been at the bathroom door. When their visit ended, she commented, "Well, at least they are friendly." On another visit, she came out of the bathroom and asked if the wind chimes in there would ring. "Sure, if the window is open, they will ring," Nadine responded. "Then how come they are ringing with the window closed?"

One night, Nadine and her daughter, Deanna, were cooking supper. Catrina, her granddaughter, was playing the organ. Deanna suddenly turned to Nadine and Catrina with a strange look and asked what they said to her. "Nothing," they both replied. Deanna had the odd sensation of something, or someone, uttering to her in a transitory voice as it went by.

Later that night, the family was sitting in the radio room, watching television. Jerry asked each of them what they had said but no one had said a thing. It was the identical feeling Deanna had earlier in the evening.

The daughter of a lighthouse keeper who lived there many years ago used the museum room as her bedroom. She used to find comfort in it during severe storms. The presence of the "ghosts" there gave her a feeling of security.

When Nadine and Jerry moved to the island, they had a cat, Frisbie, which was half bobcat. Frisbie disliked the two bedrooms. One day she was sitting in their bedroom and inexplicably her hair shot straight up, she spit, hissed and shot out of the room "like a black streak."

Between tours one day, Deanna told Nadine to look at Frisbie, who was upright on her back legs, "facing the wall, batting her front paws like someone was dangling a ribbon or toy in front of her." This was not the last time they saw this.

After two years, Frisbie grew ill. In spite of her great discomfort, she would crawl up the stairway to the captain's room and lay at the base of his portrait. After the fifth time, Frisbie died. Perhaps "what she had heard so long, she now felt an affinity to," Nadine observed.

Nadine and Jerry eventually brought home two kittens, Captains Jeffrey and Samuel. One night, they were playing in the living room. Sam, inexplicably, his hair raised up like a Halloween cat, blasted through the living room, kitchen, and right through the screen door, a heavy copper screening. Sam "went through it like it was made of tissue paper."

They came upon him a few minutes later, petrified, trembling, and bleeding. Not only had he gone through the screen, he knocked two teeth loose and cut his mouth. It took months to calm him down when he entered the room. Whenever he entered, he would look about, seemingly frightened, prior to entering.

Jeffrey liked lying on a daybed in the radio room but Sam refused to do so. If you held him on the bed, Sam would watch the corner above it "frantically." Jeffrey seldom shows his claws. One evening, however, he was lying on that floor and quickly grew rigid and slithered backwards. Jerry picked him up, but Jeffrey was so scared, he clawed and scratched Jerry for no obvious reason. Jeffrey did, however, peer at the same corner that terrified Sam.[66]

OREGON

HECETA HEAD LIGHT

Located eleven miles from Florence, north of the Siuslaw River, the Heceta (pronounced "Heseda") Head Light is visible for twenty-one miles. It was built in 1894 on a cliff 256 feet above the Pacific Ocean. An active aid to navigation, Heceta Head Light is listed in the National Historic Register.

Contact: Linda Hetzler, Oregon Parks and Recreation Department, 84505 Highway 101 South, Florence, Oregon 97439. (503) 997-3851.

Hecata Head Light, *Courtesy of Walter H. Cushman*

Heceta Head was named for Captain Don Bruno de Heceta of the Spanish Royal Navy who discovered it in 1775.

Heceta House is thought to be one of the ten most haunted edifices in the United States, according to parapsychologists. In spite of its inclusion in the National Register, Heceta House garnered public notice not as a historic site but as a "ghost house." The spooky status of Heceta House has a long history, including a moment of fame when the nationally syndicated television movie production *Cry for a Stranger* was shot in and around the old structure.

Many thought the house was haunted by one or more spirits. Cupboards shut at night were found open the next morning, doors left open would slam shut, and closed windows would open. Students and groups that visited the house as part of the Lane Community College programs, described seeing something gray climb the steps of the porch, "long and flowing, almost like a puff of smoke."

Former keepers Ann and Harry Tammens assert that the spirit is benevolent. According to a previous keeper's daughter, a small cement grave marker was located on a point of land between the residence and lighthouse. The marker has since been overgrown, but it originally was the headstone of the grave of a baby girl, presumably the daughter of an early keeper.

Some say the ghost is the baby's mother, who has come back in search of her child, while others maintain it is the child herself, looking in vain for her mother.

When the Tammens took over caretaking duties at the Heceta Head Lighthouse keeper's old home, they hadn't planned on dealing with the ghost of a former resident.

"We've heard strange noises over the years," said Harry in a November 1975 *Siuslaw News* article, "Lady of the Lighthouse Baffles Workmen," sent to me by lighthouse pen pal Inspector Alan D. Zolman. The Tammens used to attribute the noises to gusty winds. They even tried rat poison, thinking they had a rodent problem. This killed a few of the creatures, but the odd sounds persisted. "On one occasion, the poison was exchanged for a seamed silk stocking in like-new condition," Harry reported.

The newspaper article speculated that the mysterious lady was no visitor in the usual sense. In fact, she could only be described as the station's "ghostly occupant."

When renovations took place, workmen were baffled by misplaced tools, lost log books, and mysteriously opened padlocks to the attics. Eerie feelings came over them while working in the upper story of the structure. Tools disappeared only to reappear later in the same spot where they had been left.

"The hair on the back of your neck would just stand on end all of a sudden and you felt like somebody was in the room watching you," said Jim Alexander, contractor for the project. "We were upstairs in the bedrooms just below the attic refinishing some doors when our sandpaper disappeared," Alexander continued. "Neither of us had gone anywhere else in the house, so we started to tear up the room looking for the paper. We looked everywhere and couldn't find it. About an hour later it appeared again on a top bunk, one which we had turned over and shook in our search."

The following week, he was working in the attic. "I was cleaning a window which looks out over the ocean, and I kept seeing things in the glass. I wiped at them but finally decided it was reflections from something outside. It was about ten in the morning and bright outside.

"I turned around and saw this elderly lady with a long gown and long gray hair watching me. She walked across the attic with her hair and gown flowing behind her. She had a very wrinkled face. She was . . . like apparitions you see in Hollywood movies, except she moved across the room without ever touching the floor . . . it seemed that her feet were about a foot off of the floorboards." The workman dove for the trap door and jumped through the opening to the second story bedrooms, some fourteen feet below, got into his work van and drove into town.

Alexander balked at coming into the attic again but finally returned to do finishing touches on the roof supports. "I climbed to the second story roof from outside the building to work this time. I avoided looking into the windows of the attic," he said.

In the midst of his work, he inadvertently broke one of the attic windows with a hammer and had to replace it from the outside, leaving the broken glass strewn about the attic floor inside where it fell.

That night, the Tammens were roused from their bed by "scraping" sounds in the attic above, but returned to sleep without investigating the sounds. The next morning, they discovered that the broken glass had been swept into a neat pile in a corner of the attic away from the window which had been broken. "We didn't even know that the window had been broken until we asked Jim later," they said.

The Tammens said that the strange scraping noises sounded like someone scraping their foot repeatedly across the floor. "Maybe she's a barefoot ghost and just didn't want to have to step on broken glass," added Ann Tammen.

Harry Tammen described a night when he, Ann, and their guests were playing cards. They were shaken by a shrill scream that sent chills down their spines. Upon investigation, they found no cause for the scream.

Jim Alexander has had dreams in which the "Gray Lady" has appeared. "I remember seeing her again in a dream and she was . . . asking me if I didn't want to come and live at her house and keep it in good repair," he shuddered. He rejects that idea but would like to have his log book back. "It has all the job specifications in it, and I really need it for my records."

The Tammens believed that the spirit was friendly and felt that they enjoyed a peaceful coexistence. They considered the ghost to be "part of the family."[67]

The "Gray Lady" also made her presence known to former care-takers Duncan and Carolyn Stockton. Duncan believes she is simply a gentle spirit who loves her house too much to leave. Most of the ghostly activities occur after there has been a commotion at the house, like the celebration of the light station's hundredth anniversary. The "Gray Lady" displayed her displeasure by making clicking sounds on the stairs, coughing quietly, opening the windows, and making lights flicker.

"She never really spooks anybody. She's been a nice lady," says Duncan, who has had his tools misplaced and found curtains on the floor. He even saw a face in the attic window on the north side of the house. Duncan and his wife are comfortable with their resident ghost and feel that she is a healing influence.

Apparently, the "Gray Lady" likes to stay home at night. She is a wispy, lonely figure who fancies sitting by her attic window and looking past the pounding surf to the lighthouse.

The late Oswald Allik, who was employed for many years in the U.S. Lighthouse Service and stayed at Heceta Head after the Coast Guard took over the service in 1939, was the last keeper of the Heceta Station prior to automation in the 1960s. He and his wife, Alice, guided courtesy tours for thousands of visitors. Invariably, the conversation would focus on the structure in which they resided and the tales of its "sinister reputation as a haunted house."[68]

When Keepers Mike and Carol Korgan were redecorating the rooms, they added an antique couch that they suspect was haunted. They had though the Portland house they lived in years earlier might be haunted because of curious tricks and events. When they sold the house and moved, they took the couch with them, but the pranks continued.[69]

TILLAMOOK ROCK LIGHT

Located on the Pacific Ocean a mile and a half off Tillamook Head and twenty miles south of Seaside in the northeast corner of Oregon, Tillamook Rock Light was built in 1881. The tower is sixty-two feet high, with the top of the lantern one hundred and thirty-three feet above the sea. Listed in the National Historic Register, Tillamook Rock Light is a columbarium, a repository for human ashes.

"Terrible Tilly," as Tillamook Rock Light is called, has an extraordinary background, as cited in this unusual item that appeared in the *New London Day* reported through the Associated Press:

> "Lighthouse Slated as Ash Repository"
> "A group of investors that bought a 100 year old, defunct lighthouse perched on a rock off the wave lashed Oregon coast says the . . . structure will become a repository for human ashes. Mimi Mirissette . . . and others formed Eternity of the Sea Columbarium, which will operate the offshore tomb.[70]

Tillamook Rock Light is a severely exposed light station. In great gales, Pacific waves have swept over the station, damaging the lantern. It is built on top of Tillamook Rock, thought to be sixty million years old, a rocky area that Native Americans believed was possessed by evil spirits.

"Early coastal Clatsop Indians looked upon the rock with awe," states *Lighthouses of the Pacific*. Natives connected it with the spirit world, speculating that clandestine, under-ocean tunnels lived in by spirits ran to the rock.

The first white men to arrive learned that the local tribesmen demonstrated "a fearful respect for the rock and never attempted to scale its slimy walls or to land their dugout canoes."[71]

Weeks prior to the laying of the Tillamook Rock Light cornerstone, twenty-five people perished when their fishing boats foundered at the Columbia River's mouth in the midst of a storm. Witnesses described seeing "a ghostly boat sail through the floating wreckage as if picking up the souls of those that died."

Tillamook keepers described low, chilling groans and howling noises from the stairwell, primarily during driving, southwesterly storms. A clammy breeze passed that felt like "being brushed by a wet blanket." In the 1950s, the Coast Guard recounted spotting a ghost ship in the fog directly below the lighthouse.

Like the Boone Island kamikaze birds that flew into the light, "hundreds of dead seabirds of many species have been observed lying below Tillamook Lighthouse when its beacon stabbed gale filled nights," keepers have noted. Their mass death remains a mystery.[72]

Tillamook Light was abandoned in 1957, the inside gutted to the bare stone blocks. Since 1980, shelves of urns hold the ashes of the dead. *The Keeper's Log* reports that, "Ashes are stored in niches in the tower. The higher up, the more costly the niche . . . nearer my God to Thee!" The former lighthouse is "the largest islet columbarium of its kind anywhere in the nation."

Blanche DeGood Lofton forever commemorated "Terrible Tilly" in *Tillamook Light 1881-1957*, which I quote in part:

> "Shorn of her light and her glory.
> Abandoned, forsaken . . . bereft;
> Deserted by tender and keeper!
> The last lone man has left . . .
> The night is so black in the west!"[73]

YAQUINA BAY LIGHTHOUSE (OLD)

Located at Newport in Old Yaquina State Park, the original Yaquina Bay Lighthouse was constructed in 1871 and decommissioned in 1874, giving it one of the briefest active careers of any lighthouse on the Pacific Coast, with only one keeper. The frame structure was abandoned in favor of the Yaquina Head Lighthouse. Listed in the National Historic Register, it houses marine memorabilia in a museum.

Contact: Friends of Yaquina Bay, 846 S.W. Government Street, Newport, Oregon 97365. (503) 265-5679.

Yaquina Bay Light (Old), *Courtesy of Sherrie Lewis-Cato*

The specter of Muriel Trevennard is said to haunt the old lighthouse. Although the Lincoln County Historical Society, which manages the lighthouse, maintains that the Muriel story is fictional, I prefer to think otherwise.

Muriel Trevennard is thought to have perished in the lighthouse under bizarre circumstances.

Over one hundred years ago, Muriel came with her father on a ship from Coos Bay. He was thought by many to be the ship's captain, and "left his daughter in care of the hotel landlady while he traveled," according to the article, "The Haunted Lighthouse at Newport by the Sea." On her own in a new town, Trevenard spent her time "sketching or taking long walks alone on the beach below the abandoned lighthouse."

She made friends with a group of campers. After a few days investigating the region, they thought it might be fun to visit the deserted lighthouse. Muriel was escorted by a young man who had been "attracted by her charm." As they walked into the lighthouse, they saw a circular wooden staircase that wound up to the second floor.

Yaquina Bay Light rear exterior, *Courtesy of Sherrie Lewis-Cato*

On that floor, they discovered a closet that contained a piece of metal covering a dark hole. It was thought to be the hollow trunk once used to drop the weights that turned the lens. The finding resulted in all sorts of speculation "and an accompanying sense of dread." They ran down the stairs and as they made their way out the front door, Muriel realized she had forgotten her gloves and went back inside the lighthouse. Her admirer beseeched her to forget them but she persisted and went back inside alone.

Yaquina Bay Light interior staircase, *Courtesy of Sherrie Lewis-Cato*

When Muriel did not return, the group thought she was playing a trick by exiting through the kitchen door at the rear of the lighthouse. Screams, "chilling cries," immediately came from the structure. The group attempted to open the front door but it was locked from the inside. Muriel was nowhere to be found. They left in dread, still wondering if she had pulled a prank.

A search party the next day attempted to locate Muriel. What they found were pools of blood on the staircase and close to the closet with the black hole. Muriel was not to be seen nor heard from ever again, nor did her father ever come back for her.

The lookout tower of the Coast Guard is situated opposite the old lighthouse. Men on duty have witnessed odd glows coming from within the old lighthouse. One time, Coast Guard personnel described witnessing the gleam of a swinging lamp nearing the watch tower. As it came closer, it looked as if a form carried the light in hand. But when they turned on the water tower floodlight to better see the form, they saw nothing there.

Many years have passed since the disappearance of Muriel Trevenard in the Old Yaquina Bay Lighthouse. There was a time local folks said, "neglect and decay made it look like a haunted lighthouse." But since the Lincoln County Historical Society has taken over Old Yaquina Bay Lighthouse, that is no longer the case.

On some nights, bizarre noises have been heard reverberating from the lighthouse. There are those who profess to have observed the ghosts "of dead keepers drifting about in the fog where once the light had shown."[74]

YAQUINA HEAD LIGHTHOUSE

Located three miles north of the Yaquina Bay entrance and built in 1873, the Yaquina Head Lighthouse is ninety-three feet high and one hundred and sixty-two feet above the sea. An active aid to navigation, the Yaquina Head Lighthouse is listed in the National Historic Register.

Contact: Michael Noack, Bureau of Land Management, P.O. Box 936, Newport, Oregon 97365.

Yaquina Head Light, *Courtesy of Walter H. Cushman*

During the construction of the Yaquina Head Lighthouse, one of the workers fell from the top of the masonry tiers, plummeting to his death between the double walls. Rather than recovering the body from the narrow niche, the corpse was allegedly entombed inside and the vents sealed, closing off any access to that portion of the structure. Ever since, his ghost has haunted the tower.

Yaquina Lighthouse is an eerie place on a windy night. Keeper John Zenor, who put in twenty-two years of duty, asserted that the place has its own ghost and attendants always accepted it as fact. He and others manning the light said they would frequently hear somebody enter the tower and come up the spiral staircase when no one was there.

Hollywood's Universal Studios perpetuated the ghostly reputation of the lighthouse in 1977 when producers of a Nancy Drew production used it as a major attraction. The premises were temporarily taken over by the movie staff after the prop crew gave the formidable tower a haunted-look makeover both inside and out.

"Everyone heard the specter," said Zenor, "but after the war [World War II], we never heard him again."

Between the Yaquina Bay Lighthouse and the tower at Yaquina Head, a resort hotel was built between Nye and Agate Beaches in the 1880s. It was constructed by Tom Briggs, who was married to a Native American woman. One night, a gale lashed the seas as he was returning to the hotel by horse. When he attempted to cross a rain-swollen creek, a breaker engulfed him and his horse and swept them to sea, never to be seen again. His daughter, upon hearing the shocking news about the loss of her father, fatally shot herself.

For years, residents of the area claimed they saw her ghostly figure walking on the beach on stormy nights in search of her father.[75]

CHAPTER V

GREAT LAKES LIGHTHOUSES

MICHIGAN

BIG BAY POINT LIGHT STATION

Big Bay Point Light Station is located on the Upper Peninsula of Lake Superior, the largest saltwater lake in the world. It is often referred to as "The Graveyard of the Great Lakes." Native Americans called it "Gitchegoome." It is twenty-seven miles northwest of Marquette. Big Bay Point Light was constructed in 1896 and utilizes a Third Order Fresnel lens. Listed in the National Historic Register, the light has been converted into a bed and breakfast.[76]

Contact: Big Bay Point Lighthouse, #3 Lighthouse Road, Big Bay Point, Michigan 49808. (906) 345-9957.

Big Bay Point Light, *Courtesy of Linda Gamble*

Michigan is the state with the most lighthouses. Big Bay Point Light Station is located on Lake Superior, the deepest of all of the Great Lakes.[77]

The first of our Great Lakes' haunted lighthouses operates as a bed-and-breakfast with seven guest rooms, all with private bath. It also features a common living room, dining room, library, and a sauna in the tower. There are no individual televisions or phones, but forty acres of woods and trails for the guests to explore. Several people have reported seeing a ghost at the Big Bay Lighthouse Bed & Breakfast.[78]

William Harry Pryor was the first keeper of the light station, arriving on August 15, 1896. Pryor had trouble maintaining assistant keepers, some thought it was because he was a workaholic. After the resignation of the second assistant keeper, Pryor's oldest son, Edward, was officially designated as the assistant keeper in 1900. Edward evidently showed many of his father's workaholic ways, "like father, like son," according to a June 22, 1901 *Marquette Mining Journal* article.

One such example was when Edward fell on the landing crib, the base of the lighthouse, and injured his leg. In spite of the fact that his injury did not properly heal, he carried on with his duties, which proved to be his undoing. The following spring, Pryor rowed Edward to St. Luke's Hospital in Marquette to attend to his injury, but it was too late. Gangrene had set in and was spreading. On June 13, William Pryor was summoned to Marquette. Edward Pryor died that morning.

After Pryor came back to Big Bay Point, he became despondent over the death of Edward and took a gun and strychnine and vanished into the woods.

The June 24 edition of the paper ran an announcement of a reward made by the Marquette Lodge No. 108 of the Odd Fellows: fifty dollars for the individual who discovered Pryor alive, or his body if he committed suicide. Pryor, when last seen, was wearing, among other items of clothing, his regulation lightkeeper's cap.

Seventeen months later, in mid November, 1902, a hunter who sat on a log to eat lunch observed what he thought was a kettle hanging in a tree about fifty feet away. Upon examination, he discovered a man's skull suspended by a three-quarter-inch rope. The black mass thought to be the embers of a dead fire was clothing that hid the skeleton.

The hunter immediately informed the authorities. Coroner Crary completed a comprehensive examination that concluded: "The skeleton was denuded of flesh but a lightkeeper's cap full of hair with a reddish hue still clung to the skull." Red was the color of Pryor's hair.

On November 19, the *Marquette Mining Journal* stated that Pryor's wife, Marie, recognized the coat and two razors discovered in the pocket as the property of her deceased husband. Will Pryor was interred where he died, a mile and half from the light station. There are those in the Big Bay region that maintain Pryor could have been murdered.[79]

Keeper Linda Gamble recounts that one night she awoke to the clamor of the kitchen cabinet doors opening and closing. Guests often went downstairs in search of a late night snack, but this time the sounds did not cease. Gamble thought it best to go to the kitchen and help the guest to locate whatever they were in search of. But the moment she opened the kitchen door, the noise stopped.

There was not a soul in the kitchen.

Linda knew it was not her imagination. She thought of accounts of ghosts who grow apprehensive when their "home" is undergoing alterations. At Big Bay Point, modifications were regularly made to keep up with the demands of a bed-and-breakfast.

Gamble said aloud: "Will, everything's under control," assuming it to be the spirit of William Pryor.

Since that time, there have been no more episodes of kitchen cabinet doors mysteriously opening and closing.

A guest stated that she was sitting in her room in front of the mirror doing her hair when the image of a man in a lightkeeper's uniform materialized in the mirror. She turned around to find no one behind her. It was not her husband playing a trick on her. He was happily snoring away, having gone to bed before her.

Shortly after the bed-and-breakfast opened, two guests reported seeing Pryor walking restlessly around the lighthouse, attired in his U.S. Lifesaving Service uniform. Other visitors have described looking out the window and witnessing a spectral form with reddish hair sauntering by the cliff's edge.

Previous owners of the bed-and-breakfast, Norman "Buck" and Marilyn Gotschall report that a cleaning woman came screaming up the stairs one day from the basement and demanded to know who was taking a shower down there.

Gotschall later remarked that the ghost was not one to waste water for he turned off the shower.

Much like Linda Gamble's experience with the opening and closing of the kitchen cabinets, Gotschall related an incident that occured on a windy night, the first night she stayed over after buying the lighthouse. Lying in bed, she heard pounding and went outside to find out the cause.

As soon as she went outside to check, the wind subsided along with the banging. The banging resumed, and she would check but never discovered anything unfastened.

She supposed it was Pryor's "welcoming committee."[80]

If Will Pryor is the ghost of the former Big Bay Point Light Station, his appearances have not hurt business at the bed-and-breakfast. They are booked solid during the summer months. In addition, it is the first haunted lighthouse bed and breakfast I have heard of that has a Web site: www.lighthousesbanb.com.[81]

CRISP POINT LIGHT

Located west of Whitefish Point on Lake Superior, Crisp Point Light's Fourth Order Fresnel lens was lit in 1904. In 1947, the light was abandoned. It is listed on *Lighthouse Digest's* Endangered List.

Where the Crisp Point Light stands today is a woebegone brick tower on the distant and deserted coast. A volunteer group, however, is making headway in saving the historic Crisp Point Lighthouse.

Crisp Point Light, *Courtesy of Carolyn Ortiz*

Prior to the beginning of the twentieth century, the light station included a duplex for the keeper and his assistant, a fog signal house, oil house, and outhouses, in addition to the lifesaving station.

In the mid-1960s, the abandoned lighthouse keeper's quarters were still upright, though long deserted. One summer night, three boys spent the night in the old structure, arriving at dusk and stomping up the battered stairs to the attic where they unrolled their sleeping bags. All lugged .22-caliber rifles, the beach being a suitable location to display their marksmanship.

After dark, when they bedded down for the night, the boys made out the dense stomp of weighty footsteps ascending the steps, and finally reaching the landing at the head of the stairs. They took aim with their rifles, letting loose a hail of bullets.

There was not a sound from the stairs.

The boys waited, guns aimed. Finally, two fell asleep, the other too spooked to do so. All continued silent, until just prior to dawn when he heard a sound. The boy shook the others awake and they all heard someone turning at the top landing and escaping down the stairs.

Crisp Point Light was named for Christopher Crisp, a renowned lifesaving keeper of the point's first station. Could the ghost have been the specter of Crisp studying the invaders at his light? Or maybe the ghost of a prior keeper? Or, just perhaps, the apparition might have been one of the many seamen who drowned along the bleak shore?[82]

POINT AUX BARQUES LIGHT

Located on Point aux Barques Reef on Lake Huron, Point aux Barques Light stands eighty-nine feet high. It was first lit in 1848, and was rebuilt in the mid-1850s. Listed in the National Historic Register, Point aux Barques Light is an active aid to navigation with a museum located in the keeper's quarters.

Contact: Lighthouse County Park, Port Hope, Michigan 48468.

A manager is hired during the summer to maintain the grounds around the lighthouse and lives in the assistant keeper's quarters, which is more roomy and comfortable than the old 1857 keeper's house, now used as a museum.

Many years ago, the manager's daughter stayed with her parents in the old assistant keeper's house. In the middle of the night, she awoke to a strange noise. Sensing a presence, she opened her door and peered into the dark hallway, but saw nothing. She moved cautiously to the head of the stairs and gazed down. Suddenly, she was overwhelmed by a sensation of soothing tranquillity. Instinctively, she knew everything was all right.

At the foot of the steps, glistening faintly, was the well-defined, nearly solid ghost of a woman from another era. She seemed thin and of average height, and she wore a long, old-fashioned dress with an apron tied around her waist. Neither old nor young, she exuded a celestial timelessness. Her left hand lingered on the banister and she did not speak or move.

The daughter had an overpowering feeling that the woman had been the old keeper's wife, that she had come from the first keeper's quarters to investigate the happenings in the new house.

The daughter, prior to meeting the ghost, was always anxious when she visited the light, with an awareness of dread. But after meeting the apparition, she regarded the light as soothing and calm, and anticipated her visits.[83]

POINT IROQUOIS LIGHT

Located on Whitefish Bay on the eastern shore of Lake Superior, Point Iroquois Light was first operational in 1871. It is listed in the National Historic Register and is currently a museum within the Hiawatha National Forest.

Contact: Point Iroquois Light Station, Route 1, Box 344, Brimley, Michigan 49715. (906) 437-5272.

Point Iroquois Light, *Courtesy of Audrey Lutes Edwards*,

Deserted by the Coast Guard in 1965, Point Iroquois Light was taken over by the U.S. Forest Service. To aid in the upkeep of the light which now functions as a small museum, the Forest Service, in collaboration with the Bay Mills-Brimley Historical Research Society, utilizes unpaid custodians.[84]

One custodian from 1984-86 was DeVerna Hubbard. During the summer of 1985, Hubbard met a woman she has not seen since who requested permission to walk the grounds. Baffled, Hubbard said yes and guided her around the area.

The woman ventured down a path in the direction where the first light stood. According to *Haunted Lakes*, she halted between a grove of trees, turned to Hubbard and said: "A little girl was killed here and a bear carried her up the hill."

The woman said she was a psychic, never having been to the light before.

After walking 75 feet from the first location, she stopped and said: "A little girl was killed right here, killed by a bear."

Hubbard noted that when the psychic said this, she was growing colder, goose bumps appeared on her arms. She was shivering, in spite of it being an unusually warm day, close to 80 degrees.

Later Hubbard discovered that a little girl had been killed by a bear near the light and it carried her body up a nearby hill. When locals later hunted and killed a large bear on the hill, the remains of the child were found in its stomach.

A Native American legend of 1662 tells of a great war party of Iroquois traveling from the lower lakes, planning to capture the great Ojibway campground at Sault Ste. Marie. They took a break at the point that would later carry their name and made ready for the attack and commenced a great war dance. But the Ojibway had seen them advancing and made ready with an ambush.

Ojibway scouts assumed animal forms and entered the Iroquois camp, discovering that to make ready for battle, the attackers would dance nonstop for four days and nights, until they fell with exhaustion.

On the fourth day, the Iroquois fell into a deep sleep. In the hours before dawn, the Ojibway crept silently into the camp, attacked and slaughtered them all. The victors saved two braves but at a terrible price. They cut off their noses, ears, fingers and toes, gave them some food, and sent them crawling home to let the Iroquois nation know of the overwhelming Ojibway power.

The Ojibway butchery was not complete until they lopped off the heads of the dead braves and set them on poles all along the Lake Superior beach. The gruesome pickets ran for half a mile. As legend tells the story, the blood from the fresh skulls dripped onto the rocks below, staining them red. Today, red-colored rocks, supposedly the result of Iroquois blood, can still be found along the shore.

The spirit of the Point Iroquois massacre is still strong. Three hundred years after the massacre, local Native American children still don' t play on the beach. Their elders call it "Naouenigoing," or "the place of Iroquois bones." There are no houses or trees along this haunted stretch of Lake Superior, only the restless spirits of the Iroquois.[85]

On a mid-November afternoon, DeVerna's sister, Zelma, was walking her dog in an area by the beach. DeVerna was away for the weekend and Zelma was assuming her duties as caretaker. Zelma and her dog walked where the slaughter took place more than three hundred years prior. Zelma later said that while wandering the shore, "the low moaning wind sounded eerily like human voices."

She leaned into the wind, and both Zelma and her dog were struck with a burst of cold air. The dog's back hair stood on end, and it instantly returned to the safety of the light, abandoning Zelma on the barren beach. She, too, immediately returned to the light, and didn' t dare go outside again that night.

Others at the light describe curious events. Some say they have made out heavy footsteps on the spiral tower stairs, but upon investigation, there no one was there. An October 19, 1985 entry in the lighthouse log by Zelma reports: "I'm sure we have a ghostly resident here at times. I slept very little."

PRESQUE ISLE LIGHTHOUSE (NEW)

Located on Lake Huron and constructed in 1870, the new Presque Isle Lighthouse is visible twenty-five miles out in Lake Huron. The tallest tower on the Great Lakes at one hundred and thirteen feet high, the light utilizes a Third Order Fresnel lens, is an active aid to navigation, and is listed in the National Historic Register.

Contact: 4500 E. Grand Road, Presque Isle, Michigan 49777. (517) 595-2059.

This haunted light involves a keeper's wife who "got in the way," according to former Keeper Dan McGee. A lightkeeper's lust produced at least one ghost, a wailing woman who inhabits the "new" Presque Isle Light on Lake Huron.

Her husband was said to have found a girlfriend nearby. When he would go to town to fool around, the keeper would lock his wife in the tower for safekeeping and eventually murdered her to end her complaining. He explained her sudden absence from the station by claiming that she had returned to her family in the South.

Former keeper Dan McGee maintains that the keeper's wife, from repeated imprisonment, went insane. As a result, the keeper cemented her up in a tunnel beneath the station grounds.

According to legend, his victim chose to remain in the tower, at least in spirit, to torment her husband and others with her long spells of crying and moaning. On windy nights, a woman's screams are heard wailing throughout the lighthouse.[86]

PRESQUE ISLE LIGHT (OLD)

Located on Presque Isle Island, near Alpina in Lake Huron, the Old Presque Isle Lighthouse is listed in the National Historic Register.

Contact: 5295 East Grand Lake Road, Presque Isle, Michigan 49777.

The following story is dedicated to the memory of my mother, Mary, who believed in putting the porch light on to guide you home.

Presque Isle translates to "almost an island" in French. The lighthouse and the keeper's cottage are among the oldest structures on the Great Lakes, built in 1840. The light served for only thirty short years before it was replaced by the taller, further reaching Presque Isle Lighthouse built only a mile away.

Patrick Garrity, the last keeper, was appointed by President Lincoln and assumed command of the new light in 1871. The old lighthouse was abandoned and fell into disrepair until the Stebbins family took possession of the property around the turn of the twentieth century. They restored the facility, turning the cottage into a museum that is still open to the public.

Lorraine and George Parris, a quiet, retired couple, moved in as caretakers for the museum in 1977. They had lived there for two years and were on their way home one night when they noticed the light's beam over Lake Huron. The Stebbins family had restored the lighthouse to full operational status with an electric light behind the giant Fresnel lens. The Parrises thought that the current owner, Jim Stebbins, had inadvertently turned on the beacon before returning to his home.

Regardless of how it was turned on, the Coast Guard was determined to see it turned off. Running an uncharted light is not only a navigational hazard, it is also illegal. As a result, the bulb was removed and all electricity to the tower disconnected and disabled. The back half of the Fresnel lens was removed along with the motor that rotated the mechanism.

Everything was quiet at the station for thirteen years. In the winter of 1992, George Parris died of a heart attack at the lighthouse and Lorraine continued to live in the caretaker's cottage. That year, the mysterious beacon of the old Presque Isle Light was first seen. The beacon was not intensely bright, more of a dull glow, but it was bright enough to be clearly seen across the bay on the back side of the island and even by passing freighters on the lake.

Throngs of ghost watchers now park along the road, waiting for the mystery beacon, as it has become known, to show itself. Many attempts have been made to untangle the mystery. People who have entered the tower while the light is visible from across the bay find nothing in the light chamber itself. Many ghost hunters have quickly exited the tower after experiencing an unsettling feeling. Some maintain that they heard footsteps on the stone stairs behind them.

Local authorities as well as the Coast Guard have been called in to explain the light but, as of yet, haven't determined its point of origin. There are those who reason that it is the phantom of lightkeeper Garrity, come back to the original location of his duties.

Lorraine Parris, however, believes it is only her late husband, George, "letting her know that everything is all right and keeping her company until she joins him." Anytime she would venture out alone in the evening, George would tell her that "he'd put a light in the window for her."[87]

SAGINAW RIVER (RANGE REAR) LIGHT

Located at the entrance to the Saginaw River, the Saginaw River (Range Rear) Light was first lit in 1876 and is listed in the National Historic Register.

Saginaw River Light, *Courtesy of Carolyn Ortiz*

The light tower is thought to be haunted by a lightkeeper who perished at the station. Before he died, he cautioned his family to carry on in his place, to steadfastly keep the light burning, to keep a never-ending vigil over "his" light. They took him at his word and faithfully kept the light burning.

When the Coast Guard took over from the Lighthouse Service, thunderous repetitions of footfalls on the old circular iron stairway leading up the tower were said to be heard. But upon being investigated, the stairs were inevitably empty.

In the 1960s, two Coast Guardsman were keeping a late watch in the light. One kept watch while the other napped. In the early morning hours, the sleeping man was awakened by the watch stander.

"Something is in the tower," the horrified sailor stammered, according to *Haunted Lakes*. Together, they neared the tower door. They could distinctly make out the slow thudding of heavy boots ascending the stairs inside, but an oversized padlock still fastened the heavy steel door.

Could it have been the old keeper, or his family, constantly keeping the light burning?[88]

STANNARD ROCK LIGHT

Located off Keweenaw Peninsula in Lake Superior, thirty-two miles northeast of Big Bay Point, Stannard Rock Light was first lit in 1882, and features a Second Order Fresnel lens. It is listed in the National Historic Register.

The region around the Stannard Rock Light is known for curious, strong magnetic disturbances that can throw ships' compasses wildly off their marks. Piloting the area in fog with an unreliable compass is particularly frightening and exceptionally hazardous.

The building of Stannard Rock Light first began in 1878. The crib and the stone tower were constructed on the Skankee shore, fifty-five miles from the reef, using stone blocks quarried from Kelley's Island on Lake Erie. The work was arduous. The total construction cost of $305,000. was considered exorbitant for that time. Many of the blocks weighed thirty tons. In 1882, the $254,000 lens was lit.

Thought to be one of the most isolated locations in America and one of the bleakest sites on the Great Lakes, Stannard Rock Light is the furthest from land of any lighthouse in the United States. It is completely exposed to the sweep of Lake Superior, and the tower is sometimes jarred by the force of the crashing waves, despite its approximate weight of 240,000 tons. Wave spray often soars over the lantern room, one hundred and ten feet above the lake.

It was not atypical, upon opening the light in the spring, to have to hack through ten feet of ice just to get into the tower. Keepers were taken off the stations at the close of the shipping season, usually around December 1. One year the light wasn't ready for business until July. Stannard Rock Light was originally manned by a Lighthouse Service civilian skipper, who had the highest pay of any lightkeeper in the country due to the challenge of manning Stannard Rock Light.

When the Lighthouse Service and Coast Guard merged in 1939, military Coast Guardsman pulled duty at the rock, sometimes contemptuously referred to as "Stranded Rock," according to *Haunted Lakes*. Initially, the light was serviced by the civilian keepers of the Lighthouse Service.

Although never formally acknowledged, it was long thought that assignment at the rock was often used as punishment by the Guard.

In the old days when light crews maintained their own boats, it was three weeks at the rock and one off. Gravely disturbed by the loneliness, one Coast Guardsmen was said to have been removed in a strait jacket and sent quickly to a hospital.

In 1944, when the light was electrified, power was provided by four large generators installed by the Coast Guard in the coal-fired boiler house. The generators used extremely explosive gasoline.

Four Coast Guardsmen were stationed there when the light was being automated, including an electrician's mate to fix one of the generators. Shortly before 9:30 p.m. on June 18, 1961, one of the men was asleep in the fourth floor seaman's quarters, two others in the second floor galley, and the fourth was supposedly on duty in the watch room. Instead, he was in the old boiler house beside the stove.

Suddenly the lighthouse was jolted by an immense blast that shot up from the engine room through the tower. The two men were blown across the room, one badly burned. The third man, asleep in his bunk, was thrown onto the floor. Smoke and flames were everywhere. The three men retrieved jackets, a tarp, and two cans of beans, and fled outside as far away from the burning engine room as they could get. They huddled together under the tarp and awaited rescue in the freezing weather.

Eighteen hundred gallons of gasoline had blown sky high in an enormous fireball, in turn lighting the coal in the bunker. Hot clouds of smoke rose like a giant chimney. Everything was incinerated.

Rescue took two days. The survivors were sure that when a passing freighter reported that the 156,000 candlepower light was out, or that the usual radio checks with Manitou Island or Marquette were not made, someone would be quickly dispatched to investigate. But nothing happened until 11:30 p.m. on June 20. The Coast Guard buoy tender *Woodrush* learned of the catastrophe when it made its customary two-week supply run. The *Woodrush* extinguished the fire, which was still burning, and rescued the dazed survivors. The only trace ever found of the fourth man, the watch stander who ventured into the engine room, was his key ring.

What caused the blast was never known. There was a theory, however, that the man on watch, a habitual pipe smoker, opened the door to the engine room and his smoldering tobacco met with the room's heavy gas fumes, causing an explosion to rip through the air.

The Coast Guard in 1962 completed automating the rock. The inside was gutted and the old lighthouse was left a lonely, empty shell. Later, solar-powered weather monitoring equipment was added. Today the light is shut tight, only visited by Coast Guard maintenance crews.

The light is a scary place often surrounded by thick Lake Superior pea soup fog. Land is never in sight. With shipping lanes seventeen miles to the north, even freighters are infrequent.

Since the blast, Coast Guard crews have been adverse to serving the light any time near night or daybreak, only wanting to do the job during daylight. Even then, the site has a peculiar, ominous feel to it. Following the blast, workers in the lighthouse have described an overpowering feeling of not being alone. Coast Guardsmen surmise the fourth man is still on the light and they want no part of him.

Maybe the soul of a civilian keeper who served the light is holding the spirit of the careless smoker a prisoner at the light in retaliation for destroying it?

Whatever it is, the abandoned old light is not a place the Coast Guard crews want to visit. As one of them said: "It's just too spooky."[89]

ST. JOSEPH NORTH PIER INNER LIGHT

Located at the entrance to the St. Joseph River on Lake Michigan, St. Joseph Light North Pier Inner Light was first illuminated in 1907.

Job depots were established to serve the lights by dispensing timely repair, maintenance and supply services. St. Joseph's was an active depot until 1917, when it was closed. In 1919, the facility, conveyed to the Navy Department, was used by the naval reserve for many years. In 1952, it was utilized by the Army Reserve and taken over in 1956 by the Michigan Army National Guard as an armory. In 1993, the National Guard abandoned the site.

Supernatural happenings have been reported in the bulky, sinister-looking three-story brick storehouse and the smaller keeper's house. Although long-abandoned, they are still thought to be structurally sound. The inside of the job depot is a wreck. Windows are boarded over, walls punched through by vandals, stairs rotted through, and dust piled high. According to *Haunted Lakes,* a wind from the right direction can set up an eerie moaning sound that echoes eerily through the depot's empty room. Weird cold spots can be felt, and visitors sense that they are not alone.

The National Guard unit housed assorted supplies in the first floor of the house. As such, the Guardsmen had to enter the house many times a year, but no one ever volunteered for that job. On at least two occasions, odd noises were heard coming from upstairs that sounded like someone muttering: "Get out. Just leave me alone."

It was also not uncommon to leave equipment in one room and then find it in another. Some describe strange lights in the old house.

Is it the ghost of a former keeper still inhabiting his old home?[90]

STURGEON POINT LIGHT

Located on Sturgeon Bay/Lake Huron, the Sturgeon Point Light was erected in 1869, is listed in the National Historic Register, and is currently used as a museum featuring furniture and decor from the 1870s.

Contact: Don Sawyer, P.O. Box 252, Harrisville, Michigan 48740. (517) 724-5056.

Frederick Stonehouse, when researching *Haunted Lakes* at the Sturgeon Point Lighthouse Museum, writes that upon entering the structure, the hair on the back of his neck instantly began to "tingle." Instinctively, he felt ill-at-ease and was aware that he was not alone.

He came into a room on the second floor outfitted as a display area. A long light switch on the wall by the door controlled the electric lights in the case. Stonehouse switched it on, quickly inspected the display, and, finding nothing of interest for his book, turned the light off.

From another wall, he took down many Lifesaving Service photographs for duplicating and brought them down to his camera in the living room. When he came back with the photos, the display case light was switched on. Once again, he turned the light off, experiencing a feeling of dread. The hair on the back of his neck tingled and a cutting blast of cold rolled up his back. Later, when he returned to the display room the case light was on again. Stonehouse once again switched the light off, quickly collected his camera equipment, and left the building.

Museum employees have had a hard time turning the lights out. After closing for the day, sometimes they opened the next morning to discover lights burning they were sure were turned off the night before.

Stonehouse speculates it might be the specter of first keeper Percey Silverthorn to this day maintaining the light.[91]

THUNDER BAY ISLAND LIGHT

Located at the southeast end of Thunder Bay Island on Lake Huron, east of Alpena, Thunder Bay Island Light was first lit in 1832 and raised ten feet in 1857 to its height of fifty feet. Thunder Bay Island Light is listed in the National Historic Register and is an active aid to navigation in a national wildlife reserve. One of the oldest lighthouses on the lake, the brick keeper's quarters were added in 1868.

During the 1930s and '40s, Thunder Bay Island Light was said to be haunted by the ghost of an old lightkeeper known only as "Morgan."

"Morgan" is thought to still walk the forlorn shore of the island. His appearance spooked Coast Guardsmen from the island's lifeboat station during their lonely night patrol. Young surf men who patrolled the beach on the lookout for ships in distress, barely catching sight of him in their peripheral vision, often said he followed them.

Since the light was automated in 1980, the island had been deserted. But could Morgan's ghost still be wandering this deserted scene?[92]

WAUGOSHANCE LIGHT

Located northwest of Waugoshance Island, sixteen miles west of the Straits of Mackinac on Lake Michigan, Waugoshance Light was completed in 1851. The tower is seventy-six feet high with walls five feet thick at the base and stands seventy-six feet tall. The light may have housed the First Fresnel lens on the Great Lakes and was the first lighthouse on the lakes to be built on a submerged crib. Decommissioned in 1912, the tower is listed in the National Historic Register and *Lighthouse Digest's* list of endangered lighthouses.

Located on an especially dangerous reef and island ranging about seven miles out into Lake Michigan with a water depth of twelve feet or less, the area is a graveyard of wrecks.

During the 1940s, the Waugoshance Light area was placed "off limits" to civilians to provide naval aviators with bombing practice, particularly with heat seeking missiles. Apparently, the light was hit by a stray missile and the fire that resulted destroyed the interior of the tower.

There are said to be two ghosts at the lighthouse.

During the construction of the crib, a worker was killed and his spirit is said to haunt the light. When conditions are just right, the wind blowing in hard and cold, his hideous cries are said to echo across the lonely shore.

Waugoshance Light was rendered antiquated by the New White Shoals light in 1910, but locals claim otherwise. They maintain that Waugoshance was closed because it is haunted by the ghost of a keeper who died there in 1894.

John Herman, keeper from about 1885-1894, drowned at the light station. He drank heavily while on shore leave, and he stayed drunk for several days after returning to duty. His assistant lit the lamp one evening at sunset and found himself locked in the map room, a victim of one of Herman's practical jokes.

The imprisoned man called down to Herman, drunk and staggering along a pier, but Herman disappeared. According to local gossip, from then on strange things began to happen. If a keeper fell asleep on duty, his chair was kicked out from under him. Doors would mysteriously open, or worse, get closed and locked. Some unseen being reportedly shoveled coal into the boilers. All of these incidents were presumably the handiwork of the mischievous ghost of Johnnie Herman.

Though the name "Waugoshance" probably originated from Native American tongue, the light is often referred to as "Wobbleshanks," thought to be derived from the distinctive "wobble" walk of the intoxicated keeper, heading toward his doom off the pier.[93]

WHITE RIVER LIGHT STATION

Located at White Lake Channel on Lake Michigan, White River Light Station was lit in 1875 and is an active aid to navigation.

Contact: (Summer only) 6199 Murray Road, Whitehall, Michigan 49461. (616) 894-8265.

White River Station Light, *Courtesy of Carolyn Ortiz*

When Karen McDonnel, director/curator at the White River Light Station Museum first moved into the lighthouse, she was aware that the previous curator believed it was inhabited by good spirits, according to *Haunted Lakes.*

Captain William Robinson, an English immigrant, arrived at White River in the 1860s and saw the need for a functioning light to serve lake mariners. Until one was built, he took it as his personal responsibility to keep a welcoming beacon burning at the end of an old pier. Congress authorized $10,000 for the project and the lighthouse was completed in 1876.

Robinson became the first keeper and served faithfully for forty-seven years. He and his wife, Sarah, raised eleven children, two dying in childhood. Sarah was a wonderful mother and well-respected in the community. When she died at a relatively young age, it was a blow for Captain Robinson. He clung even closer to "his" light.

In 1915, at age 87, Robinson was forced by the government to re-tire, but was able to arrange to have his eldest grandson, Captain William Bush, named keeper in his place. William Bush served twenty-six years, until the light was inactivated in 1941.

Old Captain Robinson proceeded to do much of the work of tending the light, asserting that his grandson, in spite of being the keeper, was not yet ready. Slowed by age, he needed a cane to get around, but still carried on his office much as he always had. Captain Robinson lived there with his grandson despite government regulations mandating that only the keeper and his immediate family live in the building. As the day drew closer for his farewell, Robinson grew depressed. For nearly fifty years, his life had been the light, particularly after his wife's death.

Finally, he told his grandson: "I am not going to leave this build-ing." The morning he was to leave, he died. In accordance with his wishes, the old Captain was buried in the small cemetery across the river so he could be as close to "his" light as possible.

About a month after McDonnel completed an investigation on Cap-tain Robinson for her job as curator, she made out the distinct sound of someone walking upstairs on the second floor. Slow, hesitant, faltering steps were accompanied by a periodic thud. McDonnel thought it was the old keeper. Today, the odd upstairs pacing occurs on a regular ba-sis.

"The walking I heard is as if someone were checking . . . I feel it is a ritual and that I shouldn't disturb it. It's calming," McDonnel stated.

During a trip away from the lighthouse, McDonnel turned over its care to a couple who agreed to house sit. She made no mention of the captain's walk. When she returned, her house-sitting friend said: "Do you have some kind of ghost walking around upstairs?"

Her friend described the same sounds of walking upstairs. While the eerie noise did not scare the house sitter, they did make her anxious and uncomfortable.

McDonnel wonders if the presence is the old captain checking on the children, walking down the hall looking into each room, then slowly climbing the iron spiral stairs up to the lamp room for a final check of the light. She thinks Captain Robinson values the extra work she does at the light.

Below the lamp room, at the top of the spiral staircase, there is window set deep into the octagonal outer wall outfitted with a wooden resting board. McDonnel claims that many have felt a strong draw or appeal in that area, as if a presence were seated on the board.

Maybe it was the old captain's custom to pause at the window after checking on his sleeping children.

McDonnel discovered that Captain Robinson's wife, Sarah, helped with the lighthouse in addition to her mothering duties to their eleven children. When the keeper was ill, she cared for the light in his place.

Karen McDonnell has located several pictures of Sarah, and is especially fond of a charcoal drawing that appears to have a unique presence about it. When she placed Sarah's photos on display, McDonnel felt she was praising a very special lady.

Upstairs, in what had been a children's room, is a large, flat glass display case holding assorted artifacts. The top of the case is a dust magnet and needs to be cleaned every other day. One day, after she'd hung Sarah's pictures on the wall, McDonnell was dusting the display case. The phone rang and she put the rag on the corner of the case and quickly took the call. She was worried that it would soon be opening time and she didn't want visitors to find the rag on the case. After the call, she ran back upstairs, and, to her surprise, found the display case dusted. There were no open windows and the rag was now on the other side of the case.

"That gave me a chill," McDonnell recounted. "How could the cloth move itself the other side without wind . . . Since I've brought Sarah back into view, maybe she is helping me." Later, when no one was in the museum, McDonnel said aloud: 'Thanks Sarah.' She has continued to play the game with her. Five minutes before opening, she'll place the rag on the case and go back downstairs.

Sure enough, when McDonnell returns, the rag is not where she left it and the dusting is done. She wonders if, in addition to Sarah wanting to help, maybe it has to do with the fact that Sarah's younger children's bedroom was located in the room where the display case is now.

McDonnel is not disturbed that her light is haunted. "I like the . . . comfort it gives me . . . like a watchman, just making sure that everything is okay."[94]

MINNESOTA

SPLIT ROCK LIGHT

Located on the north shore of Lake Superior in a state park, Split Rock Light was erected in 1910. It rises one hundred and seventy-eight feet above Lake Superior and is listed in the National Historic Register.

Contact: Lee Radzak, Minnesota Historic Society, 2010 Highway 61 East, Two Harbors, Minnesota 55616. (218) 226-6372.

Our only Minnesota haunted lighthouse was featured on the Great Lakes Lighthouse stamps series issued by the United States Post Office. It is also the site for the annual commemoration of the November 10, 1975 sinking of the *Edmund Fitzgerald*, wherein all hands, twenty-nine men, lost their lives in "the winds of November." The commemoration is the only time when the light is open at night.

Weather is so brutal around Split Rock that it has been said if you plan to visit the site after October, be prepared to stay for six months, for you probably will not be able to leave until the thawing rays of spring melt the heavy ice and snows. Wolves have been heard to howl outside the lighthouse at night.[95]

The first two assistant keepers based at Split Rock in 1910 drowned in Lake Superior when the boat they were taking to town for mail capsized. The boat was discovered on the shore, but the assistant keepers were never located.

Our first story of spectral happenings at Split Rock took place in the mid-1980s and has several variations in the retelling.

After closing for the day, a visitor found he had lost his wallet. He promptly came back to the tower structure where he thought it might be and began pounding on the door. There was no answer. Irritated, he walked back and looked up to the lamp room. Watching over the railing and eyeing him right back was an elderly gent dressed in lightkeeper's attire. He did not respond to the visitor's request to be allowed back in or to queries concerning his wallet.

When he again glanced at the locked door, the visitor observed that it was padlocked from the outside. He pondered what the man at the railing was doing locked in the tower.

The visitor departed. Upon returning the next day, he recovered his wallet, but never discovered who the odd keeper was. Museum guides sometimes dress in period costume, but no one confessed to being in the tower when the visitor was there.

The second account is somewhat different.

After beating on the museum door for some time, it abruptly opened. A man in keeper's attire silently gave the visitor his lost wallet (or camera?), said not a word, and rapidly closed the door and vanished. Once again, the next day, the museum staff did not know anything about the event.

Could the old man in the keeper's uniform be one of the assistants who drowned in 1910?

Situated on the grounds are three, two-story dwellings first lived in by the keeper and his two assistants. The middle structure is presently lived in by the resident curator.

About ten years ago, while in her bedroom dressing for dinner, the curator's wife noted an extremely powerful perfume aroma in addition to an intense sensation of being watched. There was no one about and no logical reason for the smell of perfume.[96]

NEW YORK

OSWEGO HARBOR WEST PIERHEAD LIGHT

Located at the mouth of Oswego River on Lake Ontario, the site of the Oswego Harbor West Pierhead Light dates from 1822, but the tower was erected in 1934. Flashing an osculating red light every four seconds, the light is an active aid to navigation. There is no admittance but viewing only.

The Oswego Harbor West Pierhead Light not only features a ghost story, but Fort Oswego contributes a chapter to the history of the United States.

Fort Oswego has stood guard at the mouth of the Oswego River since the 1700s. The French controlled Oswego in 1654, the British in 1722. During the French and Indian War, the French regained control in 1756. The British took it back in 1776 prior to the American Revolution. The fort was surrendered to the Americans in 1796 under the Jay Treaty. The British attacked the fort during the War of 1812, but failed to capture the site. In 1814, they succeeded in destroying the fort.

The current Fort Oswego was built around 1840 and was an important site of military training and activity during the Civil War. The fort was also a major link in the famed Underground Railroad that aided escaped slaves in their flight north into Canada and freedom. Many of their descendants spend their vacations retracing the route of their fleeing ancestors. Several routes travel through Fort Oswego. Between 1944-1946, the fort was used to shelter European refugees, victims of the holocaust.

In 1942, an early winter blizzard stormed for days, marooning the solitary lighthouse keeper at his post with shrinking supplies. Eight Coast Guardsmen from the local station made out in a long boat to assist the keeper. They reached the lighthouse, leaving a replacement keeper and supplies at the station. When they piloted their boat back towards the shoreline, a sudden great wave crushed their craft against the lighthouse base. Six of the eight drowned.

From then on, the tone of odd cries and footfalls have been heard in the stairwells of the lighthouse. Malfunctioning lights are regularly discovered, a result of unscrewed bulbs. From the shore, lights are often seen illuminating every window in the lighthouse, even windows that were sealed over with steel plating.[97]

OHIO

FAIRPORT HARBOR WEST BREAKWATER LIGHT

Located on Lake Erie at the Grand River entrance, Fairport Harbor West Breakwater Light was erected in 1925. It is listed in the National Historic Register and is an active aid to navigation.

Contact: Fairport Historical Society, 129 Second Street, Fairport Harbor, Ohio 44077.

Fairport Harbor West Breakwater Light, *Courtesy of Carolyn Ortiz*

A tiny "puff of gray" has been spotted on the second floor of the old keeper's house, now a maritime museum, the oldest on Lake Erie.

In 1989, Pamela Brent, curator of the museum, resided on the second floor of the former keeper's house, now a small apartment. One night as Brent prepared supper, she saw "something small and dark flit by the kitchen door" and vanish down the hallway heading to the living room, according to *Guardians of the Lights*. Brent stepped into the kitchen doorway and peered anxiously down the hallway, but saw nothing there.

She returned to the kitchen. A moment later, Brent observed "a little gray cat, almost like a puff of smoke, scurrying around the floor. Its eyes were small iridescent gold marbles, its fur was thick and feathery." Oddly, "the elfin cat had no feet," moving "about the floor at the opposite end of the hallway as if propelled by invisible wheels." It appeared to be pursuing something, ran into the living room, and vanished.

Brent met the tiny apparition many times that winter, even playing with it by flinging "a balled-up sock into the hallway, which it scampered after with kitten-like joy." Brent never felt fearful or menaced by it. The ghostly kitten was friendly and appeared only to be seeking out a playmate.

When Brent researched the source of the spectral kitten, she discovered the following:

Captain Joseph Babcock, keeper of the light for forty-eight years, had come to his post in 1871. During Babcock's time as keeper, Mrs. Babcock grew quite ill and had to take to her bed for many months. While recuperating, one of her joys was a gray kitten that scampered about the upstairs rooms and gave hours of entertainment for the bedridden women. Mrs. Babcock's favorite game with the kitten was to pitch a tiny, soft ball from her bed. The kitten would chase it happily, retrieving the ball in its mouth.

Brent was aware that her apartment living room was previously an upstairs bedroom in the old keeper's house, most likely the one in which Mrs. Babcock convalesced. But Brent was not able to learn the name of the kitten or what became of it. If the tiny spectral kitten Brent played with was also the gray kitten who aided in Mrs. Babcock's recovery, it is possible it perished prior to reaching "cathood."[98]

WISCONSIN

CHAMBERS ISLAND LIGHT

Located in the middle of Green Bay on Lake Michigan, Chambers Island Light was first lit in 1868 and is listed in the National Historic Register. Standing sixty-eight feet above Lake Michigan, its Third Class Fresnel Lens has a range of sixteen miles. In 1961, the Coast Guard relocated the light from the old stone tower to a new sixty-foot steel tower, placing the beacon ninety-seven feet above water.

Contact: Joel and Mary Ann Blahnick, 9171 Spring Road, Fish Creek, Wisconsin 54212. (414) 868-3100.

The ghost of the Chambers Island lighthouse first came to note in 1976 when caretaker Joel Blahnick arrived. At the time the lighthouse was in bad shape, having been deserted for more than twenty years. The facility was to be upgraded for a planned four-acre town park and museum.

The first night Blahnick spent in the lighthouse, he awoke to a loud booming sound. Heavy footfalls coming down the spiral staircase emanated from the lamp room. The heavy footsteps traveled down the hallway, through the living room, down the steps into the kitchen, and to the outside grounds. The kitchen door closed behind the specter with a distinct "click."

If others visiting the light openly doubted the ghost's existence during the day, it was sure to wake the doubters during the night. Non-believers were frightened into consciousness by the loud footsteps and an overpowering sensation of an unearthly presence.

The spirit was always congenial, at times playful. During the summer of 1979, it acted like a poltergeist. Tools and other items vanished, only to be found later in unlikely locations. When Blahnick and his father were working on a window, a screw driver placed on the sill "went missing." Later it was found under a pillow in the bedroom.

In 1987, the haunting ended. A group of nuns from a local retreat took a tour of the lighthouse and grounds. After the director
related the tale of the supernatural activities of the light, one of the
nuns, walking briskly to the outer side of the building, placed her
hands firmly against the old brick tower wall and prayed for the
spirit's release from its earthly bounds. After a minute, she stopped
and returned to the group. Whatever she said was apparently effec-
tive. The ghost has not returned since.

Although there was no hard evidence as to the identity of the
spirit, Blahnick thought it was the first lightkeeper, Lewis Williams.
His twenty-two-year tenure was the longest of any of the island's
keepers, enough to sire eleven children while tending faithfully to
the beacon.

Before the light was built, Williams operated a sawmill at the
northwest point of the island. When Congress decided in 1866 to
construct a lighthouse on the island, it was Williams who, for the
sum of $250, sold the property to the government, managing to have
himself appointed as a keeper for $50 a year. He tried several times to
have his wife appointed assistant keeper, but without success.[99]

CHAPTER VI

CANADIAN LIGHTHOUSES

COVE ISLAND LIGHTHOUSE

Cove Island Lighthouse is located on northern Lake Huron in Georgian Bay, Ontario.

Cove Island Light is well known to sailors as a check-in point in the renowned Port Huron to Mackinac Sailboat Race.

This ghost story involves Captain Tripp, a man of the sea. Tripp's small boat, the *Regina*, was his glory. He took on cargo at the Goderich dock one September morning in 1881, choosing between two cargoes, salt or wood. It was a fateful decision that he chose salt.

When the *Regina* rounded Cape Hurd, she ran into a wild gale. But it was the salt that really proved to be the *Regina's* undoing. It soaked up water, vastly increasing the weight of the *Regina*, taking away the ship's buoyancy with every breaking wave.

"As the *Regina* rode lower, the waves punished her more, causing her seams to open further and allowing the salt to absorb more of the cold lake waters," according to an article in *Great Lakes Cruiser*. Tripp was sure he could make it to a sandbar off Cove Island by the lighthouse and beach the *Regina* where she could wait out the gale. But the crew was not so convinced. They mutinied in the only lifeboat, abandoning Tripp to solely man the old boat in the rising storm.

Captain Tripp never did make it to the sandbar. An inquiry following the wreck of the *Regina* revealed that both the boat and Tripp could have survived had they remained afloat just a few moments more. The *Regina* sunk in the shallows off Cove Island, her masts barely touching the Georgian Bay surface. Captain Tripp's body was never recovered. Local rumor, however, maintains that he was interred on Cove Island close to the lighthouse.

Many years after, a comparable autumn gale to that which took Captain Tripp roared over the area around Cove Island. Locals recalled that: "In desperation, freighter captains searched the whirling white blindness for the familiar beacon of the Cove Island Lighthouse that would set their bearings."

It blazed normally in the early part of the gale but was quickly put out. Ships and men were at the mercy of the storm and the maze of rocks off Cove Island. To everyone's relief, the light once again glowed, directing the ships around the hazards.

But when the Lighthouse keeper was queried about the relighting of the light, he was of little help. He was in town during the incident, having lit the lamp and locked the tower before he left, not caring to be in the tower alone during such storms. In his words, "The autumn storms bring strange happenings to Cove Island Light."[100]

GIBRALTER POINT LIGHT

One of the oldest lights on the Great Lakes and the first erected on Lake Ontario, Gibralter Point Light is located at the southwest corner on Centre Island that forms the southern flank of Toronto Harbor. First lit in 1808, the tower stands eighty-two feet high. The light was discontinued in 1959.

Some islanders believe that the spirit of the first keeper, J.D. Rademuller, who served from 1808-16, still haunts the lighthouse. Visitors report reverberating footfalls echoing through the old structure. Others claim to hear his unearthly moans. Moving shadows cannot be explained and odd glowing clouds add to the idea of a spectral keeper.

It has been said that Rademuller was murdered during a drunken quarrel with soldiers from nearby Fort York. Rademuller, a faithful and fastidious recent German immigrant, was the perfect keeper. The lighthouse was always clean and well ordered, everything in place.

He did like his beer, though, and coming so recently from Germany, his brewing skills were sharp. It was well known that he made the best pilsner on the lake. Fort York, a small fort or blockhouse, was also located at Gibralter Point and soldiers often visited the keeper for conversation and beer.

On January 2, 1816, three soldiers, already drunk, showed up at the lighthouse and demanded beer. Noticing their drunken state, the lightkeeper declined to give them any.

Rademuller attempted to cool them down and encouraged them to go back to the fort. But they wanted beer. One soldier wielded a piece of firewood like a club and demanded more beer or else!

When the keeper again protested, the soldier's arm swung down and the makeshift club hit the keeper sharply on the side of the head, knocking him to the floor. Still infuriated, the men dragged his unconscious body to the top of the tower and threw him to his death. To hide proof of their crime, they sliced the keeper to pieces and entombed the pieces all over the grounds. Another account relates that they beat him to death with their belts.

The soldiers fled and the secret of the keeper's whereabouts went unsolved. Authorities appointed a Mr. Halloway in his stead.

Sometime after 1832, Keeper James Durnam found bones while digging near the light. Authorities thought them to be those of the missing keeper, that he had been murdered. Durnam later said that on dark and foggy nights, he not only heard the old keeper's wails, but also saw his ghost looking in vain for his murderers.

This is an instance where the specter ghost provided tangible proof of his presence. The inside of the tower was covered with either plaster or whitewash. A newspaperman thought he would spend a night in the lighthouse to unmask the spectral legend. He inspected the light early in the evening and discovered nothing out of the ordinary. During a later examination, he observed "rubbing from the plaster walls at shoulder height" and wondered if a specter created the rubbing. He also found some plaster had peeled onto the steps, layering them with a fine white powder, according to *Haunted Lakes*.

Incapable of sleep as a result and wanting to move along the dark hours of the night, the frightened man cleaned the steps. Later, when he again checked them, there was more white powder, this time stamped with enormous footprints.

At the beginning of the twentieth century, old lake captains frequenting Toronto Harbor thought the ghost was still in the lighthouse. They called him "the old man" or "old man Muller," the murdered keeper.[101]

CHAPTER VII

BAHAMIAN LIGHTHOUSES

GREAT ISAACS LIGHT

Located on Great Isaacs Island, Bimini, sixty miles off the coast of Florida, the Great Isaacs Light features fifteen horizontal bands of red and white.

"Oh! dream of joy! is this indeed
The light-house top I see?"
(Samuel Taylor Coleridge, "Rime of the Ancient Mariner")[102]

Years prior to the construction of the lighthouse, a hurricane hit the island, resulting in many shipwrecks and personal tragedies in our last story.

Following the storm, wreckers and salvagers from Bimini went out on the beach to see what they could claim as their own. Two brothers who had been sailing in the area landed on Great Isaacs Cay. They found the remains of a wrecked ship strewn upon the shore as well as human remains scattered about the beach.

The brothers found the body of a woman with a baby in her arms. The woman was dead, but the baby had endured the two days that had passed since the storm. The men attempted to extract the infant from the rigor mortis grip of the mother. Ultimately, they had to slip the baby out of its clothing to release it. They swaddled the child in their own clothing and left the remains of the woman on the shore, still gripping the infant's garb.

Once home, the brothers' mother knew the baby needed prompt attention. The baby subsequently survived, was adopted and lived in Bimini for many years.

Some time after, the British Government sent a ship to Great Isaacs Cay with sections of the disassembled Great Isaacs Light aboard. At that time, beacons were commonly constructed in England and shipped all over the world. Workers delivered the parts ashore and put them together.

Months later, when the lighthouse was almost finished, a worker standing on the beach observed what seemed to be a woman. According to Ken Black's *Shore Village Museum Newsletter*, she wailed a low moan in a faltering voice, trying in vain to locate her missing child. The worker dashed into the house where his fellow workmen were gathered. He related what he had witnessed and heard.

Soon thereafter, the foreman of the construction crew walked down to the water's edge. He started back toward his quarters and was amazed to see a woman walking in a furtive manner, repeating the moaning cry.

From that night until the lighthouse was completed, August 1, 1859, the Phantom Lady of Great Isaacs was seen by one workman after another. When the lighthouse was completed, the work gang left the island, but not before they had warned the keepers about the Phantom Lady.

From 1859 until 1913, the Phantom Lady made an appearance. Some of the keepers related their run-ins with the lady. Usually, they detected her walking the shore where the child had been found in her arms at the time of the hurricane. Appearances were always in the light of a rising moon.

In 1913, the keeper recounted that the Phantom Lady tried a new tactic, ascending the lighthouse steps.

One night, as the keeper was walking down the tower's spiral staircase, he beheld a form below slowly walking up toward him, ascending the lighthouse steps. When she was only two turns on the spiral steps below him, he could hear her wailing out, in search of her missing infant.

The keeper was unable to move up or down. The woman drew closer until she was only one turn on the spiral staircase from him. He spun around and raced up the stairs into the turret, slammed the trap door, and moved a massive crate of machinery over it. And there he stayed until dawn. Afterward, he requested a transfer to another lighthouse.

The new keeper arrived in 1914, resolute about freeing the island of the ghost. The next day, he officiated over an internment ceremony at twilight in the area where the remains were discovered. His genuine spiritual air and manner of humility affected all at the service. The feeling of the island seemed more livable instantly after the ceremony ended.

Since the service, the lady has never re-materialized. Many believe she was the supernatural entity of the dead mother, forever searching for her baby.[103]

BIBLIOGRAPHY

Addams, Charles J., III. *New York City Ghost Stories: Chilling, True Encounters with the Supernatural in the World's Most Exciting and Haunted City.* Reading, Pennsylvania: Exeter House Books, 1996.

Altman, Kimberly. "Discover Why Georgetown County is Called . . . The Ghost Capital of the United States." Georgetown, South Carolina: Georgetown Chamber of Commerce flyer.

Beck, Horace. *Folklore and the Sea.* Mystic Connecticut: Mystic Seaport Publications, 1996.

Big Bay Point Lighthouse brochure, Big Bay, Michigan.

Black, Ken. "Isle of Shoals Light: Interesting History." Rockland, Maine: *Shore Village Museum Newsletter,* November 5, 1996.

Bolte, Mary. *Haunted New England.* Riverside, Connecticut: The Chatham Press, Inc., 1972.

Boston Daily Journal, April, 1851.

Coleridge, Samuel Taylor. *Rime of the Ancient Mariner.* New York: Dover Publications, 1970.

De Wire, Elinor. *Guardians of the Lights: Stories of U.S. Lighthouse Keepers.* Sarasota, Florida: Pineapple Press, Inc., 1995.

-------. *Guide to Florida Lighthouses.* Sarasota, Florida: Pineapple Press, Inc., 1987.

-------. "Winged Visitors-Birds at Lighthouses." Wells, Maine: *Lighthouse Digest,* December, 1995.

"Discovering Michigan Presents: Ghosts & Guardians of Lake Superior." Grand Blanc, Michigan: *The Outdoor Journal,* 1994, video tape.

Eckels, Donald and Robert Fraser. "Minots Ledge." San Francisco, California: *The Keeper's Log,* Fall, 1995.

Edwards, Jack. "The Hard-to-Please Lightkeeper." Royal Oak, Michigan: *Great Lakes Cruiser,* October, 1995.

Ellis, Edward and Elaine Amass. "Murder at the Lighthouse: Government "Cover Up." Wells, Maine: *Lighthouse Digest,* March, 1995.

Ertle, Lynne. "Heceta House." Wells Maine: *Lighthouse Digest,* October, 1996.

Farrant, Don. "The St. Augustine Lighthouse-Heritage and Strange Happenings." Wells Maine: *Lighthouse Digest,* August, 1998.

Galgan, Ignatius J. "1867 Long Island Sound NO ZIP Code." Wells, Maine: *Lighthouse Digest,* July, 1996.

Gibbs, James A. *Lighthouses of the Pacific,* West Chester, Pennsylvania: Schiffer Publishing Ltd., 1986.

"Gurnet Light Tower Saved from Attack by the Sea, Plymouth, Massachusetts." San Francisco, California: *The Keeper's Log*, Spring, 1999.

Hacker, David. "Bed, Breakfast, Ghost: Inn keeping with spirit of Lighthouse." Detroit, Michigan: *Detroit Free Press*, Sunday, October 29, 1989.

"Haig Point: At Home on Daufuskie Island." Hilton Head Island, South Carolina: Haig Point information packet.

Hamilton, Harlan. *Lights and Legends: A Historical Guide to Lighthouses of Long Island Sound, Fishers Island Sound and Block Island Sound*. Stamford, Connecticut: Wescott Publishing Co., 1987.

Harper's New Monthly Magazine, April, 1861.

Harrison, Timothy and Betty Bowman. "The Doomsday Lighthouse of Sabine Pass." Wells, Maine: *Lighthouse Digest*, April, 1997.

Harrison, Timothy. "Cape Hatteras Lighthouse: Day of Reckoning approaching?" Wells, Maine: *Lighthouse Digest*, September, 1995.

Harvey, Karen. "Phenomena." *The Compass*, May 24, 1990.

Hauck, Dennis William. *The National Directory of Haunted Places*. Sacramento, California: Athanor Press, 1994.

"Haunted Lighthouses Across the U.S." *The Learning Channel*, broadcast October 25, 1998.

"Haunts of the Great Lakes . . . The Old Presque Isle Lighthouse, Grand Lake, Michigan." Royal Oak, Michigan: *Great Lakes Cruiser*, October, 1994.

Hawthorne, Nathaniel. *Passages from the American Note Books of Nathaniel Hawthorne*. Boston, Massachusetts: Ticknor & Fields, 1868.

Holzer, Hans. *Hans Holzer Haunted America*. New York: Barnes & Noble Books, 1993.

Huntsinger, Elizabeth Robertson. *Ghosts of Georgetown*. Winston-Salem, North Carolina: John F. Blair, 1995.

"*In Search of* . . ." NBC television series, May 13-15, 1976.

Jenvey, Bruce. "Captain Tripp Lights The Way." Royal Oak, Michigan: *Great Lakes Cruiser*, October, 1994.

-------. "Oswego, Gem of the Far East." Royal Oak, Michigan: *Great Lakes Cruiser*, October, 1994.

"Lady of the Lighthouse Baffles Workmen." Florence, Oregon: *The Siuslaw News*, November 26, 1975.

Lanigan-Schmidt, Therese. "Ghostly Past Beams on State's Lighthouses." Dearborn, Michigan: *Michigan Living*, October, 1997.

-------. "The Lighthouse Steps." Davis Park, New York: *The Fire Island Tide*, June, 1993.

"Lighthouse Slated as Ash Repository." *New London, Connecticut: New London Day*, c. 1981.

"Lighthouses of Long Island -- An Exhibit." San Francisco, California: *The Keeper's Log,* Summer, 1999.

Lofton, Blanche DeGood. "Tillamook Light 1881-1957." San Francisco, California: *The Keeper's Log,* Fall, 1996, inside back cover.

Lynch, Tom. "Legend of Theodosia." Charlotte, North Carolina: *Charlotte News,* 1947.

Marquette, Michigan: *Marquette Mining Journal,* June 22, June 24, and November 19, 1901.

"Memorial for heroic keepers given "OK." *Lighthouse Digest,* February, 1998.

Miller, Lischen M. "The Haunted Light at Newport by the Sea." Newport, Oregon: *Pacific Monthly,* Vol. II, 1899, reprinted by the Lincoln County Historical Society, Pub. No. 10, 1973.

Myers, Arthur. *The Ghostly Register: Haunted Dwellings-Active Spirits, A Journey to America's Strangest Landmarks.* New York: Contemporary Books, 1986.

New Haven, Connecticut: *New Haven Register,* June 28, 1983.

"New Keepers at Point Iroquois," Wells, Maine: *Lighthouse Digest,* December, 1995.

O'Brien, FitzJames. "Minots Ledge." *Harper's New Monthly Magazine,* April, 1861.

"The Portrait." Wilmington, North Carolina: *Wilmington Home Magazine,* March, 1974.

Roberts, Bruce, and Ray Jones. *Southern Lighthouses: Chesapeake Bay to the Gulf of Mexico.* Old Saybrook, Connecticut: Globe Pequot Press, 1995.

Roberts, Nancy. *Georgia Ghosts.* Winston-Salem, North Carolina: John F. Blair, Publisher, 1998.

-------. *South Carolina Ghosts: From the Coast to the Mountains.* Columbia, South Carolina: University of South Carolina Press, 1983.

Sargent, Colin. "Inside Boon Island Light." Wells, Maine: *Lighthouse Digest,* December, 1995.

Seguin 200: 1795-1995. Friends of Seguin Island.

Snow, Edward Rowe. *Famous Lighthouses of America.* New York: Dodd, Mead & Company, 1955.

Snow, Edward Rowe. *The Lighthouses of New England, 1716-1973.* New York: Dodd, Mead and Company, 1973.

Stonehouse, Frederick. *Haunted Lakes: Great Lakes Ghost Stories, Superstitions and Sea Serpents.* Duluth, Minnesota: Lake Superior Port Cities, Inc., 1997.

Thaxter, Celia. *Among the Isles of Shoals, Boston.* Massachusetts: Houghton Mifflin Co., 1873.

Thomas, John Rogers. "The Cottage by the Sea," 1850.

Thompson, William O. *The Ghosts of New England Lighthouses.* Salem, Massachusetts: Old Saltbox Publishing and Distributing Inc., 1993.

Tugel, Nadine A. "Battery Point Lighthouse: Ghosts Dragons Mermaids." pamphlet.

Ufford, Rev. E. S. "Take Good Care of the Light." Wells, Maine: *Lighthouse Digest*, February, 1998.

Verde, Thomas A. *Maine Ghosts and Legends: 26 Encounters with the Supernatural*. Camden, Maine: Down East Books, 1989.

Williams, Docia Schultz. *Ghosts Along the Texas Coast*. Plano, Texas: Republic of Texas Press, 1995.

INDEX

ENDNOTES

[1]Thompson, William O., *The Ghosts of New England Lighthouses*, Salem, Massachusetts: Old Saltbox Publishing & Distributing, Inc., 1993, pages 15-17.

[2]Excerpted from: *Folklore and the Sea*, by Horace Beck, published by Mystic Seaport Publications, 75 Greenmanville Avenue, Mystic, Connecticut 06355, 1996, page 181.

[3]Thaxter, Celia. *Among the Isles of Shoals*, Boston, Massachusetts: Houghton Mifflin Co., 1873.

[4]Sargent, Colin. "Inside Boon Island Light." Wells, Maine: *Lighthouse Digest*, December 1995, page 29.

[5]DeWire, Elinor. "Winged Visitors - Birds at Lighthouses," Wells, Maine: *Lighthouse Digest*, December 1995, page 13.

[6]*The Ghosts of New England Lighthouses*, op. cit., pages 29, 31.

[7]*The Ghosts of New England Lighthouses*, op. cit., page 26.

[8]"Paddling Inn to Inn in Maine, "Wayne Curtis, New York, New York: *The New York Times*, July 13, 1997, page 10.

[9]Holzer, Hans. *Hans Holzer Haunted America*, Barnes & Noble Books, New York, 1993, pages 165-181.

[10]From the book *Guardians of the Lights: Stories of U.S. Lighthouse Keepers*, copyright ©1995 by Elinor De Wire. Used by permission of Pineapple Press, Inc., Sarasota, Florida, page 89.

[11]*Guardians of the Lights*, op. cit., page 114.

[12]*Folklore and the Sea*, op. cit., pages 138-139.

[13]"Take Good Care of the Light," Rev. E.S. Ufford, Wells, Maine: *Lighthouse Digest*, February, 1998, page 29.

[14]*The Ghosts of New England Lighthouses*, op. cit., pages 15-17.

[15]"Ghosts on Seguin," section of booklet, pages 30-31, sent by Webster-Wallace, Anne, April 10, 1995.

[16]*The Ghosts of New England Lighthouses*, op. cit., pages 21-24.

[17]*The Ghosts of New England Lighthouses*, op. cit., page 8.

[18]Ken Black. "Isles of Shoals Light: Interesting History:" Rockland, Maine. *Shore Village Museum Newsletter*, November 5, 1996, page 5.

[19]Hawthorne, Nathaniel. *Passages from the American Note Books of Nathanial Hawthorne*. Boston, Massachusetts: Ticknor & Fields, 1868.

[20]Bolte, Mary. *Haunted New England*, Riverside, Connecticut: The Chatham Press, Inc., 1972, pages 55-58.

[21]Verde, Thomas A. *Maine Ghosts and Legends: 26 Encounters with the Supernatural*, Camden, Maine: Down East Books, 1989, pages 21-26.

[22]*The Ghosts of New England Lighthouses*, op. cit., pages 19-20.

[23]"Gurnet Light Tower Saved From Attack by the Sea, Plymouth, Massachusetts," San Francisco, California: The Keeper's Log, Notice to Keepers, Spring, 1999, page 31.

[24]*Guardians of the Light*, op. cit., pages 40, 134-135, 186.

[25]"Haunted Lighthouses Across the U.S.," cable television broadcast on October 25, 1998, *The Learning Channel*, 10 P.M.

[26]*Guardians of the Light*, op. cit., pages 247-248. O'Brien, FitzJames. "Minots Ledge," *Harper's New Monthly Magazine*, April, 1861.

[27]Eckels, Donald & Fraser, Robert. "Minots Ledge," San Francisco, California: *The Keeper's Log*, Fall, 1995, page 2.

[28]"Minots Ledge," op. cit., page 8.

[29]"Minots Ledge," op. cit., page 2.

[30]Snow, Edward Rowe. *Famous Lighthouses of America*, New York: Dodd, Mead & Company, 1955, pages 64, 66.

[31]Snow, Edward Rowe. *The Lighthouses of New England,* 1716-1973, New York: Dodd, Mead & Company, 1973, page 222.

[32]"Memorial for heroic keepers given 'OK,'" Wells, Maine: *Lighthouse Digest,* February, 1998, page 7.

[33]*Guardians of the Lights,* op. cit., page 255.

[34]"Minots Ledge," op. cit., page 16.

[35]Hamilton, Harlan. *Lights & Legends: A Historical Guide to Lighthouses of Long Island Sound, Fishers Island Sound and Block Island Sound,* Stamford, Connecticut: Westcott Cove Publishing Company, 1987, pages 189-190.

[36]Meyers, Arthur. *The Ghostly Register: Haunted Dwellings - Active Spirits, A Journal to America's Strangest Landmarks,* New York: Contemporary Books, Inc., 1986, pages 63-68.

[37]*Lights & Legends,* op. cit., pages 74-79.

[38]*Lights & Legends,* op. cit., pages 27-31.

[39]Galgan, Ignatius J. "1867 Long Island Sound NO ZIP Code," Wells, Maine: *Lighthouse Digest,* July, 1996, pg. 5.

[40]"Lighthouses of Long Island - An Exhibit," San Francisco, California, "*The Keeper's Log,*" Summer, 1999, page 35.

[41]Lanigan-Schmidt, Therese. "The Lighthouse Steps," *The Fire Island Tide,* Davis Park, New York: June, 1993.

[42]Charles J. Adams, III. *New York City Ghosts Stories: Chilling, True Encounters with the Supernatural in the World's Most Exciting - and Haunted - City,* Reading, Pennsylvania: Exeter House Books, 1996, pages 81-85.

[43]*The National Directory of Haunted Places,* Dennis William Hauck, Sacramento, California: Athanor Press, 1994, page 95.

[44]*Guardians of the Lights,* op. cit., pages 242-244.

[45]Ray Mitchell, Donna. Letter, February 16, 1995.

[46]Ray Mitchell, Donna. Letter, February 23, 1995.

[47]Lynch, Tom. Letter, June 23, 1999.

[48]Harrison, Timothy. "Cape Hatteras Lighthouse: Day of Reckoning approaching?" Wells, Maine: *Lighthouse Digest*, September, 1995, page 1.

[49]Lynch, Tom. Charlotte, North Carolina: *Charlotte News*. "Legend of Theodosia," op. cit.

[50]Nancy Roberts. *Georgia Ghosts*, Winston-Salem, North Carolina: John F. Blair, 1998, pages 61-67.

[51]*Guardians of the Lights, op. cit., pages 234-237.*

[52]Cushman, Walt. Letter, January 24, 1996. Altman, Kimberly. "Discover Why Georgetown County is Called...The Ghost Capital of the United States." Georgetown, South Carolina: Georgetown Chamber of Commerce flyer.

[53]*Ghosts of Georgetown*, op. cit., pages 3-12.

[54]"Haig Point: At Home on Daufuski Island," Hilton Head Island, South Carolina: Haig Point information packet.

[55]Cushman, Walt. Letters, 7/31/95 and 9/27/95.
Roberts, Nancy. South Carolina Ghosts: From the Coast to the Mountains, Columbia, South Carolina: University of South Carolina Press, 1983, pages 42-53.

[56]Reprinted from *Southern Lighthouses: Chesapeake Bay to the Gulf of Mexico*, ©1983 by Bruce Roberts with permission from The Globe Pequot Press, Old Saybrook, Connecticut, 1-800-243-0495, www.globe.pequot.com, pages 81-82.

[57]From the book *Guide to Florida's Lighthouses*, copyright c 1987, by Elinor De Wire. Used by permission of Pineapple Press, Inc., Sarasota, Florida, pages 71-73.

[58]De Wire, Elinor. Letter, July 24, 1995.
Volpe-Healy, Joyce. Letter, September 30, 1995.

[59]Johnson, Sandra. Letter, September 12, 1995.
Ortiz, Carolyn. Letter, September 29, 1995.

[60]Ellis, Edward and Amass, Elaine. "Murder at the lighthouse: Government "Cover-Up." Wells, Maine: *Lighthouse Digest,* March, 1995, page 1.

[61]Farrant, Don. "The St. Augustine Lighthouse - Heritage and Strange Happenings." Wells, Maine: *Lighthouse Digest,* August, 1998, pages 15-16.

[62]Chambers, Cullen. FAX, February 15, 1995.
Harvey, Karen. "Phenomena," *The Compass,* May 24, 1990, page 8.
The Learning Channel, "Haunted Lighthouse Across the U.S.," op. cit.

[63]Williams, Docia Schultz. *Ghosts along the Texas Coast,* Republic of Texas Press: Plano, Texas, 1995, pages 160-161.

[64]Timothy Harrison and Betty Bowman. "The Doomsday Lighthouse of Sabine Pass," Wells, Maine: *Lighthouse Digest,* April, 1997, pages 17-19.

[65]Harrison, Timothy and Bowman, Betty, "The Doomsday Lighthouse of Sabine Pass," ibid.

[66]Voleck, Hazel J. Letter, June 28, 1995.
Tugel, Nadine A. "Battery Point Lighthouse: Ghosts, Dragons Mermaids," Pamphlet.

[67]Zolman, Inspector Alan D. Letter, July 4, 1995.
"Lady of the Lighthouse Baffles Workmen." Florence, Oregon: *The Siuslaw News,* November 26, 1975, page 1.

[68]Gibbs, James A. *Lighthouses of the Pacific,* West Chester, Pennsylvania: Schiffer Publishing Ltd., 1986, pages 31-33.

[69]Ertle, Lynne. "Hecata House," Wells, Maine: *Lighthouse Digest,* October, 1996, pages 30-31.

[70]"Lighthouse Slated as Ash Repository," New London, Connecticut: *New London Day,* "c. 1981."

[71]*Lighthouses of the Pacific,* op. cit.

[72]*Lighthouses of the Pacific,* op. cit., page 28.

[73]Lofton, Blanche DeGood. "Tillamook Light 1881-1957." San Francisco, California: *The Keeper's Log*, Fall, 1996, inside back cover.

[74]*Guardians of the Lights*, op. cit., pages 245-247.
Miller, Lischen M. "The Haunted Light at Newport by the Sea." *Pacific Monthly*, Vol. II, 1899, reprinted by Lincoln County Historical Society, Pub. No. 10, 1973.

[75]*Lighthouses of the Pacific*, op. cit., page 30.

[76]Videotape, *Discovering Michigan Presents: Ghosts & Guardians of Lake Superior*, Grand Blanc, Michigan: the Outdoor Journal, 1994.

[77]Stonehouse, Frederick. *Haunted Lakes: Great Lakes Ghosts Stories, Superstitions and Sea Serpents*, Duluth, Minnesota: Lake Superior Port Cities, Inc., October 1997, page 69.

[78]Big Bay Point Lighthouse brochure, Big Bay, Michigan.

[79]Marquette, Michigan: Marquette Mining Journal, June 22, June 24, and November 19, 1901.

[80]McGee, Dan. Phone interview, April 28, 1995.
Hacker, David. "Bed, Breakfast, Ghost: Inn keeping with spirit of lighthouse," Detroit: Michigan: *Detroit Free Press*, October 29, 1989, page 3A.

[81]Biggs, Jerry. Letter, January 30, 1996.
Edwards, Jack. "The Hard-To-Please Lightkeeper," Royal Oak, Michigan: *Great Lakes Cruiser*, October, 1995, pages 42-44.
Lanigan-Schmidt, Therese. "Ghostly Past Beams on State's Lighthouses," Dearborn, Michigan: *Michigan Living*, October 1997, page 12.

[82]*Haunted Lakes*, op. cit., pages 35-37.

[83]*Haunted Lakes*, op. cit., pages 7-9.

[84]"New Keepers at Point Iroquois." Wells, Maine: *Lighthouse Digest*, December, 1995, page 16.

[85]*Haunted Lakes*, op. cit., pages 37-40.

[86]McGee, Dan. Phone interview, op. cit.

[87]"Haunts of the Great Lakes...The Old Presque Isle Lighthouse, Grand Lake, Michigan." Royal Oak, Michigan: *Great Lakes Cruiser,* October 1994, pages 42-43.

[88]*Haunted Lakes,* op. cit., page 15.

[89]*Haunted Lakes,* op. cit., pages 41-46.

[90]*Haunted Lakes,* op. cit., pages 28-30.

[91]*Haunted Lakes,* op. cit., pages iv and v.

[92]*Haunted Lakes,* op. cit., page 16.

[93]*Haunted Lakes,* op. cit., pages 21-22.

[94]*Haunted Lakes,* op. cit., pages 23-28.

[95]*Guardians of the Lights,* op. cit., pages 57, 59.

[96]*Haunted Lakes,* op. cit., pages 40-41.

[97]Jenvey, Bruce. "Oswego: Gem of the Far East." Royal Oak, Michigan: *Great Lakes Cruiser,* October 1994, pages 36-39.

[98]*Guardians of the Lights,* op. cit., pages 255-257.

[99]*Haunted Lakes,* op. cit., pages 16-18.

[100]Jenvey, Bruce, Review. "Captain Tripp Lights The Way." Royal Oak, Michigan: *Great Lakes Cruiser,* October 1994, page 45.

[101]Biggs, Jerry. Letter and attachments, op. cit.

[101]*Haunted Lakes,* op. cit., pages 2-4.

[102]Coleridge, Samuel Taylor. *Rime of the Ancient Mariner,* New York: Dover Publications, 1970, page 54.

[103]Black, Ken. Rockland, Maine: Shore Village Museum. Letter, March 6, 1996.